THE GREEN B
t
OUTDOOR

2nd Edition

by
Don Paul

Super-illustrations by:
Leslie Paul
Great Photography by:
Tom McLaughlin

Fun to write; should be fun to read, too.
Hope you enjoy...

Pathfinder Books are not as good as the venison I roasted after going hungry for three days. But they're real close...

This is the second edition of the highly successful and well reviewed
THE GREEN BERETS GUIDE TO OUTDOOR SURVIVAL

ISBN: 0-938263-05-6
PATHFINDER PUBLICATIONS
COPYRIGHT 1985 & 87

Ideas aren't free. They require 10% inspiration and 90% perspiration. Our systems are unique, and require hundreds of hours to learn, work out, and write about. This book wasn't written in ink, the scars on our shins and a few broken bones are what really produced it.

Write for a free catalog of this book's brother volumes:
PATHFINDER PUBLICATIONS, HAMAKUA CENTER/SUITE 401,
150 HAMAKUA RD, KAILUA, OAHU, HAWAII 96734
Your comments are always appreciated.

The all New....
GREEN BERETS' GUIDE TO OUTDOOR SURVIVAL
2nd Edition

TABLE OF CONTENTS

BOOK ONE OF
A FOUR BOOK SERIES

THE GREEN BERETS' GUIDE
to
OUTDOOR SURVIVAL

2nd Edition

HELP WANTED: OUTDOOR WRITERS
          Who can we get to
write the best?

        This book has been
quite popular in its first
edition---so much so that I
needed to reprint. But rather
than reprint from old plates,
I have elected to expand,
revise, and add whole new
chapters. We increased
everything but the price.
This will be our best ever.

1

Suppose you were asked to write about outdoor living and survival---would you gather your material from the Green Berets? Are the Rambo guys really that good? They just might be...

Who would you have left over if you took a group of people out of society, tested them all for intelligence, and sent the lesser intellects back into the concrete jungle? Then, after that, you took the remaining smart ones and re-tested them--- this time for physical endurance. Once again, reject the losers.

After this, you have weeded out a lot of people, but the ones you have left show some promise. They have proved themselves to be smarter, stronger, and more capable than the rest. With a group like this, you have the start of something good...

Then, you teach them, toughen them, force them to endure, and their bodies. If you train them tough enough, only the individuals with enough desire and will power will succeed. Others fall by the wayside.

Even in Army jump school I was told, "Your body is about to perform far beyond what you ever thought it could do."

"What a ridiculous statement," I thought. As it turned out, my body was sacrificed to prove the truth of what they'd promised. I had never before experienced such constant pain.

After jump school, though, the training became more intense---and it never stopped. There was always another barrier to hurdle, a new level of expertise to achieve, another new skill to acquire.

2

And we practiced... Over and over again, we repeated each new move, redid old lessons, and renewed every technique until we thought it was perfect---then we did it again.

Perhaps that's why many people regard Green Berets as the foremost outdoor experts in the world. Certainly, I do. It always amazed (and also assured) me, that my fellow team members were super strong in areas in which I was weak. I've met some incredible heroes. The medic who wrote part of this book wears a silver star, and in my opinion, should be wearing several more.

COCKING ONE LEG KEEPS BACK STRAIGHT WHEN SHOOTING PRONE. RESULT: REDUCED WOBBLE.

Life has taught me that the best people in any area are those who love what they do. Like a Ray Charles in music, or an Isaac Asimov in literature, anyone who loves his work usually does an outstanding job. That's what I found in Special Forces. They love what they do---a lot. They have developed a mindset that says, "I will let nothing beat me." Every tough new challenge is a game, and as it goes in all life, it's fun to win.

Even more important is this: I don't believe I've ever encountered any group of people anywhere in the world who are more resourceful, creative, or unbeatable. Maybe it's the constant practice and training; maybe it's because they were chosen for their brains in the first place; but the methods and systems they come up with are often unbelievable.

If you can gather information from people like these, you just might write a great outdoor book, and that's what we want to publish.

Maybe that's why this four-book series has been so popular. Our COMPASS COURSE enables thousands of our readers to go anywhere and never get lost, all WITHOUT USING A MAP! Our KNIFE BIBLE has taught readers to aim their knife at the sun and tell what time it is---and the rest of the book's tricks are much better. Readers have written that GREAT LIVIN' IN GRUBBY TIMES, is the very best for teaching outdoor skills. And almost everybody laughs---because we believe learning should be fun.

*****

One night in Jan, 1976, I parachuted with my Green Beret operational detachment into the Panama Jungle. My parachute didn't open. When I pulled my reserve, it tangled with my main chute, and I began accelerating. My new, increased speed would splatter me all over the jungle. Frantically, I hauled my reserve silk back in. My main chute partially blossomed again, and as I slowed down, I tried one last, desperate time to throw my reserve into the updraft and deploy it. But I saw the darkness of the land on the horizon speeding upwards, and knew I was going to bounce--- hard.

My team medic, Rick Woodcroft, helped me stay alive. He took control, and, with God's help, brought me through.

I survived! What did it take?

PREPARATION
TRAINING
PRACTICE
WILL POWER
TEAMWORK

Not a lot. My case illustrates that. I was **PREPARED;** I had been running between eight and twelve miles every week. I executed what I was **TRAINED** to do. I **PRACTICED** parachute landing falls until they were second nature. I had **WILL POWER.** I would never give up. "You don't even think about dying; you concentrate on living!" Finally, add **TEAMWORK.** Without my medic, my injuries would have worsened. My radio operator called in help. Without my team, I might not have made it.

But that's typical. Two people working together can do far more than three working separately. The Green Berets proved that all over the world.

But why write about outdoor survival in the first place? Will it be necessary? Here's a more appropriate question: CAN HUMAN BEINGS CO-EXIST IN ANY ATMOSPHERE WHERE SELF INTEREST REIGNS ABOVE ALL ELSE?

Today, if we sing the National Anthem as it's applied, it goes, "Oh say can you see, what is in it for me?" Billy Graham calls it a "me-first" society. Non-christians call it a lack of respect for the human ethic.

I've talked to hundreds of people who believe that we are on a self-destructive down swing. Crime, drugs, pornography, teen-age pregnancy, lies, government rip-offs---all of the news appears to be rotten. Where will it stop? Even our police can't mace the nation.

Meanwhile, back on your own homestead, The seven "P" principle applies: "Proper Prior Planning Prevents Pitifully Poor Performance."

These survival manuals give you THE VERY BEST in training, practice, and preparation. Add will power to what we are about to teach you, and nobody can beat you. Come what may---any crisis, any trouble--- you'll know what to do, and----you will survive.

Listen to the counsel of Solomon, inspired by God over 2,000 years ago, when he wrote: "For by wise guidance you will wage war, and in abundance of counselors there is victory." (HOLY BIBLE Proverbs, 24:6)

Victory can be yours. Just read on.
★★★★★

PS. Incidentally, a lot of our reading customers were referred by friends. If you know someone who has an old copy of this book, THE GREEN BERETS' GUIDE TO OUTDOOR SURVIVAL please pass this word along:

"Pathfinder wants its books not only to be the best, but also the best buy on the market. So, we guarantee that your book will improve. We will upgrade these books, and supply a brand new, revised and improved book in exchange for an old copy. Send a check or money order ($4.50) along with an old, tattered cover. We'll send a brand new, updated copy, plus pay postage AND handling."

6

Section I

MAKE YOUR GUNS SPEAK
WITH ULTIMATE AUTHORITY

Introduction

THE SUPER SHOOTER
SECRETS OF ULTRA-MARKSMANSHIP

In Volume II of this series, we furnished you with a "Weapons' Attribute Chart" so you could choose the very best personal survival firearm possible. Thus, you should know exactly what's best.

Now, we're going to teach you precisely how to shoot them, precisely. These things bang out hot lead out between 500-3200 feet per second. Once the bullet(s) clear your cannon's muzzle, you have abso-God-fearing--lutely no control.

Yet, where this hot lead strikes is critical, a life and death issue-- not only for the target, but for you as well. Ask a couple of the bears I wounded recently, "How was your sense of humor?"

Wounded people are no different than wounded bears. I guarantee, you will get your target's avid attention, whether you hit or miss. If your bullet isn't well placed, the returns may well be. So--bullet placement means everything.

During the Korean war we learned that it took over 10,000 rounds per enemy kill. Vietnam was worse. I suggest you do better than that. **If you're not dead serious, don't even put your finger on a trigger. All you do when you shoot and don't hit is give away your position.** That can be a fatal mistake. Unlike politics, gunnery is not a high visibility business.

Marksmanship is the high-precision skill of causing a weapon's projectile to land exactly on target; it's a fine art form with little room for error. Lousy lawyers frequently send their mistakes to jail, and crude carpenters can paint over theirs, but a bad shot pays the full-failure price of incompetence.

You need to learn to shoot. It can be the essence of survival. Learn this skill and you can eat well, protect your livestock, or give real meaning to religious philosophy---by posting a sign that gently asks...

"Is there life after death?"
(Trespass here, and find out.)

Weapons are like tools, that is, they come in different sizes and operate best from different ranges. Because of that, we break marksmanship training into chapters; each deals with a different weapon.

8

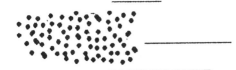

Once you can blast shot out on a level plane, your aiming problems are reduced to keeping your barrel in line with your targets.

Chapter 1

SUPER SHOTGUNNER

Shotguns are cheap, easy to use, and devastatingly effective. You can modify one to perform in tight spaces as if it were a pistol. Also, you can blast anywhere from a few to a few hundred balls or BB's and adjust the pattern to make the shot spread like water coming from the nozzle of a gardener's hose. That's versatility.

Come even decently close and you will hit--- especially if you are working around city concrete, which produces more ricochets than the romantic life of a streetwalker.

In addition, the shot load weighs over an ounce, so the close-range shock-to-target transfer is tremendous. In Book II of this series, we examined a whole bunch of different weapons' attributes, and discovered that a shotgun was your best survival bet.

Because shotguns are easier to hit with than other weapons, this chapter is much smaller than the others on shooting.

Though shotguns don't penetrate barricades very well, and they only devesate at shorter ranges, this weapon takes command on close-in, moving targets.

Two white beads on the top of the gun's rib provide the shooter with quick aim capability. Line these up, and the shot pattern will poke lots of holes in and around your aiming point.

Shooting misses occur either high/low or left/right, or a combination of both. Most commonly, shotgunners miss their target because they fail to line the sighting beads up. Since a shotgun kicks severely, it's a natural thing to keep one's face up, away from the stock. That's the mistake. Failing to keep your face in the stock is the same as elevating your rear sight, which causes the tip of the barrel to elevate. Result: you shoot over the target.

The second most common error is failure to follow through on a moving target. The shooter swings, leads, shoots--and immediately stops swinging. Result: the shot goes behind the target; it's either a clean miss, or where it hits prompts a lot more speed in the target. (You'd move out quicker too if you were poked in the rear with some hot lead.)

You want to be quick, but also accurate, so be thorough. Shooting doesn't end when the round explodes. Follow through by swinging along with the target AFTER you shoot as well as before.

In the anti-personnel mode, shotguns are often shot from the hip. Integrate the weapon into your body position, and swing the whole body left and right so the weapon traverses from one side to the other WITHOUT changing elevation.

When hip-shooting, the shot will travel in line with the gun's barrel, so, from your bird's-eye view, line the barrel up with the target to eliminate left/right misses. That's easy. The real problem, though, is eliminating high/low misses, (although low shots are effective). To get the elevation right, teach yourself how to hold the weapon in a level plane.

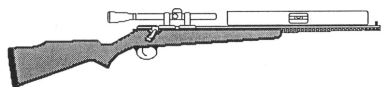

Just as you would suppose, level shots come out of a level barrel. Use a small carpenter's level on the top of the barrel's (ventilated) rib so you can tell when the barrel is level. Hold level by getting into a P-A-U-L stance. The letters stand for PLATFORM ACCURACY, UNITIZED LEVEL. A better arrangement would be: U-P-L-A, but that isn't as easy for me to remember. Nevertheless, what we are going to do is, UNITIZE-- weapon, arms and torso into a PLATFORM for LEVEL ACCURACY.

Once you've taught yourself to shoot level, you've eliminated 50% of the miss possibilities. Then, any target in line with your barrel will gain weight quickly due to lead absorption.

You lock the weapon into a level gun platform position, by forming a triangle. With finger on the trigger and your thumb wrapped over the small (pistol grip) of the stock, dig the first joint of your thumb into your hip.

THAT SPOT BECOMES
ONE, UNCHANGEABLE, UNMOVEABLE
ANCHOR POINT ON YOUR SHOOTING PLATFORM.

Then, with your left arm stiffened, hold the place on the pump handle with a cupped left hand' where the weapon lies level. Mark that spot with tape so that your <u>stiff left arm always extends to the leveling point.</u> Now, with the points on this triangle established, all you have to do is keep your back straight up and down, and fire away. Your personal gun PLATFORM will provide UNITIZED, LEVEL fire.

My favorite hip shooting practice comes from rolling old tires down a hill. Insert the side of a cardboard box inside a tire's cavity, and then roll it past the shooter. His whole body should swing and rotate, and his level weapon blasts the center out of the rubber circle. It's a real thrill, especially at night.

But thrills and fun aside, once you become a pro with this blaster, you will add immensely to your short range security.

Shot Sizes
As numbers increase, shot size gets smaller.

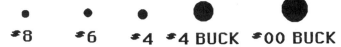

#8	#6	#4	#4 BUCK	#00 BUCK
CLAY PIDGEONS	QUAIL	DUCKS RABBITS	SMALL DEER COYOTES SHEEP	LARGE DEER WILD PIGS PRISONERS

DIFFERENT STROKES FOR DIFFERENT FOLKS..

Shotgun range increases with shot size, (better density) so load with at least four's to practice distance shots. During daytime practice, watch your misses; those puffs of dirt tell you exactly where the shot went and you correct errors that way.

To practice bird shooting, use the standard clay pigeon. The thrower stands off to the side and wings a bird across your field of fire at varying speeds. Swing with the bird by rotating at the hip, then fire and follow through by holding your lead.

Carrying your shotgun with a sling is convenient and less tiring, so adapt the shoulder strap from a canvas shoulder bag. They are long enough to support the gun in the ready-to-shoot position, and they come furnished with easy snap-on hooks.

As you will learn later, most guns are designed to be shot during the day--polite shooting hours. In a survival situation, most of your shooting will be done at night--impolitely. That's why feeling the gun in a level position is so important.

It's also a great idea to modify the top of your shotgun's rib or barrel with an iridescent white line from back dot to muzzle. Use reflector tape or fluorescent paint, and charge the line with a flashlight under a cover without looking at the light. That way you maintain your night vision, but an automatically leveled fluorescent line will point the way to a target in the dark.

With a shotgun, you really don't have to worry about precision shooting. But you have shoot from closer range in order to make your influence felt.

I hate target closeness. It sometimes causes blood loss, like mine. It's much better to let an enemy get away than it is to close in tight and experience sudden weight gain due to lead absorption. For this reason, I took the trouble and time to learn to shoot from a longer distance-- like a thousand yards away with a rifle.

First, though, we teach you to shoot a shorter, more difficult weapon to handle...

This is what happens when you focus on the target.
The front blade becomes blurry (because it's out
of focus) and therefore impossible to align sharply.
With sights only slightly out of alignment on a pistol,
the round will miss by a mile.

Chapter 2

PISTOLERO PLUS

Some tee-shirts read, "A .357 beats four aces."
Here's how to join the club...

Pistols don't scatter any shot. (exception: snake loads for .357). Pistol projectiles consist of one, rather slow moving projectile.

In the sister book to this, called, <u>GREAT LIVIN' IN GRUBBY TIMES,</u> we teach why a pistol is the last choice for a survivalist. Nevertheless, it's the most popular weapon in the United States. In Miami alone, one year's sales amounted to over $50 million dollars.

I've won several trophies and medals in pistol competition. Even so, I don't like them. Make one little mistake in shooting a pistol, and you can miss your target completely. They require **precision plus** to shoot accurately.

Only this much
sight alignment
error
will cause a clean
miss just 30° away.

Given that the weapon is inherently difficult, and knowing that the method of shooting we teach is impractical, why do we even teach pistol? Because pistol shooting principles apply to rifles. It's like teaching you to survive in the Florida swamps with nothing. Once you can do that, you can do almost anything.

More often than not, new pistol shooters fire and then discover there is no hole in their target. It's downright embarrassing to even think about, but they missed the whole target. But just look at the litany of things that could have caused the bullet to miss and fly south:

1. Bad sight alignment up/down, left/right
2. Flinch
3. Bad breath control
4. Poor trigger control / jerk /
        failure to trust your wobble
5. You heeled the pistol stock
6. Wrong stance
7. Concentration mis-focused
7. Zero out of whack
8. Weapon out (automatic bushing wear)

So--you have eight good reasons to miss. Face it; pistols are very difficult. The short sight base is not only unforgiving, it requires an eagle eye to maintain sight alignment. In addition, correct and delicate trigger squeeze is absolutely critical.

A.	B.	C.	D.
Good Sight Alignment	Disturbed. Pulled to right.	What a poor hunter gets for dinner, "trigger jerkey"	Heeled. Pistol grip forward, barrel up.

So, you marry your rear sight to your front sight good and proper. But one wrong squeeze, and she has more ways to go astray than an ex-wife

A. This is the way she looked before you pulled the trigger.
B. You pulled to the right instead of straight back.
C. Go home hungry. You jerked the trigger, down and left.
D. You pushed too hard with the heel of the hand while the hammer was falling, and the front sight rose before the bullet cleared the muzzle.

Championship pistol shooting can be achieved by following the instruction contained in one sentence: "Align the sights on the target, and cause the weapon to discharge without disturbing that sight alignment." It's easier said than done. Nevertheless, one by one, we'll eliminate each mistake.

To do that, we use a mnemonic. Think: "B-R-A-S-S." Since shell casings are made of brass, you'll have plenty of reminders. Here's what the letters stand for:

BREATHE
RELAX
AIM
SQUEEZE
SURPRISE

BREATHE. If you do it while you are shooting, you will never achieve decent bullet placement. So--stop. Breathe in a full breath, exhale, then hold it--dead still.

RELAX. I could write a volume on this one word. We teach you the outer shooting game. The inner is a biggie. For now, let's leave it this way: Make a conscious effort to relax--loosen up. Get floppy. If you tighten up a little, muscle tension and nervous shake will cause your bullets to spray all over the landscape. Tighten up a lot, and you will flinch, or jerk, which is the severest error you can make.

AIM. This little word consists of two separate and distinct activities.

A. Align the sights. Place the blade precisely in the notch nearest you. Even if you don't do it right, you must be consistent, that is, the very same each time. In pistol shooting, a sight alignment error is critical because an angle on a short base means a huge miss when the angle's lines are extended out to the point of bullet strike.

B. Obtain a sight picture. Place your **ALIGNED** sights on target. As in all shooting, focus on your sights must proceed in proper order. Pistol sight focus progression is different from rifle.

Iron sights on a RIFLE require the eye's focus to travel from:
REAR SIGHT
TO FRONT SIGHT
TO TARGET,
THEN, BACK TO FRONT SIGHT.

However, pistol sights PROPERLY adjusted for a center-of-mass hold require focus from:

REAR SIGHT FUZZY   **FRONT SIGHT SOLID**

and--severe concentration on that front sight with the target OUT OF FOCUS AND BLURRY IN THE BACKGROUND. Then, while the weapon wobbles all over the target--**BUT WITH SIGHTS ALIGNED,** squeeeeeze the trigger.

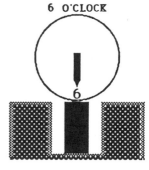

6 O'CLOCK

Let me tell you a story about sight adjustment. Most instructors teach you to picture a bullseye as if it were a clock, and take up a sight picture with aligned sights so that the bull sits right on top of your sights; in other words, aim at six o'clock. I almost got killed that way.

Two summers ago I partnered up (see Animals) with some great dogs and we chased a bear for two miles through some of Oregon's unbelievable mountain rain forest.

I arrived at the tree and the bear decides, "to hell with the dogs, I'll fight for a chance to interview this guy personally." With a roar, it reared up on a limb, and starts down after me.

Thank God I had made the extra effort to come up on the high side, (most wounded bears will charge downhill). Since the mountain was steep, the bear and I were eyeball-to-eyeball, 15 feet apart. I realized what was about to happen, so I shot, quickly, but carefully, with a good hold, a great trigger squeeze, and perfect sight alignment, and I saw the sights centered on the bear's chest as the bullet exploded. I had loaded my own .357 rounds, and this bear's heart would be history.

Well, cousin, I forgot that the pistol's zero was set for six o'clock. To compound the error, I heeled the round a bit, and my bullet went high into the bear's eye socket. But---bears' brains are protected high in the cranial cavity, so the bullet did little damage... BUT, talk about no sense of humor--WOW! Did he ever get MAD! He came ROARING out of that tree. I got off another shot, and Jim Minter shot four times, so the bear took six rounds before tangling with the dogs and running crazy. For about six more minutes, the bear duked it out with the dogs--and then died. I told everybody, just like I am telling you, that I wasn't scared a bit, but the person who does my laundry knows better.

I named this bear, Ayatolla Khomeni-- because you had to kill him to make him friendly. I had to help him smile for this picture. The name fits, cause his breath stunk and his teeth were filthy.

Six o'clock hold? Forget it. It's a terrible system because it forces a novice shooter to focus on target, and therefore the front blade is blurry. Therefore, sight alignment CANNOT BE MAINTAINED CLOSELY, and that is the kiss of death to accurate pistol shooting.

What you do is adjust your sights so that the bullet goes in right over the front blade. We call it a center-of-mass zero; that's what you use. Make sure your sights are aligned, and you can wobble all you want as long as the sights are somewhere on target. Then, keep on squeezing carefully until you are surprised by the blast.

Now think "SS." Of course, you take up the trigger slack. More than that, however, you have to apply pressure to the trigger in steady, ever increasing amounts, until the pistol surprises you as it fires. If you aren't surprised, then you know when the gun would fire, which gives you a chance to either flinch or jerk the trigger at the critical moment.

The B R A S S system is crucial to know and practice; of course, it applies not only to pistol, but rifle shooting as well.

Added to inherent pistol shooting difficulty, we begin by teaching you to shoot standing, turned sideways, with a one-hand hold. As far back as 1980, I wrote about it being a stupid way to shoot a pistol. (AMERICAN HANDGUNNER ANNUAL, 1981) Later, we will teach you a much better way to shoot. We begin by teaching this method so you learn to fire a handgun in such a way that errors are traceable to cause, and therefore correctable.

Learn this method of shooting as well as you can; it's really an important prerequisite. If you fail to learn this, then you won't know how to trace error to cause when we teach you to pop into a crouching stance and shoot in combat.

Begin by learning to hold the weapon in your hand correctly. Make a "V" with your thumb on one side and your four fingers on the other. The bottom of the "V" must point up your forearm towards you elbow.

Insert the weapon into that "V." Wrap only your middle and ring fingers around the "v" into the hand stock. Keep your little finger free of the pistol stock; it can induce error if you allow it to touch the weapon. Same with the thumb. Keep it off the weapon.

Trigger fits on finger right here.

Trigger pull must be exactly to the rear, and your sights must stay aligned after the hammer falls.

The end joint of the trigger finger presses flat against the trigger, and care should be taken during dry firing to make sure your trigger finger pulls straight to the rear. As the round breaks, you should be staring at your sights with full concentration. Memorize the way the sights looked just as the weapon fired.

Take up a stance sideways to your target. Distribute your body weight EVENLY on (unflexed) legs, shoulder width apart. Find A NATURAL POINT OF AIM, that is, place your body in relation to the target so that minimum muscle effort is required to keep your weapon on target. You need to do this with a rifle also, so learn this well.

Here's the trick. With eyes closed, raise the weapon---not to come on target, but to come to rest at your most naturally relaxed point of aim down range. Open your eyes. If the weapon is off left/right, DO NOT move your arm, but adjust your stance. Close your eyes and try it again. Repeat as often as needed. Then, once you have found your perfect, relaxed position, mark around your feet with chalk so you know exactly where to stand every time you're on the firing line.

CHALK AROUND THE FEET WILL PROVIDE YOU WITH A PERFECT RELAXED POINT OF AIM.

Finally, be careful about where you put your mind, heart and soul. Sun Duk Sun, the grand master of Tae-Kwon-Do Karate would tell you to bring your strength, mind, heart and soul to the point of impact. Do that. Focus all the concentration you have on the front sight of your weapon and squeeeze straight to the rear so that the round breaks as a surprise. TRUST YOUR WOBBLE. Don't even be concerned that your pistol seems to weave all around. Just squeeze, and, surprise!

Once you've shot several rounds, analyze your shot group. Shots all to one side mean your natural point of aim is off. Adjust it.

SHOTS INTO "JERKERS" CORNER, LOW AND LEFT.

For a right handed shooter, the lower left area of the target is referred to as "jerkers' corner."

If you can make the round break as a surprise by squeezing the trigger **STRAIGHT** to the rear, you won't jerk. Dry firing while staring at the sights is the remedy. Do this against a blank wall; otherwise you will fall into the trap of focusing on the bullseye. Watch your sights; THEY MUST REMAIN ALIGNED as the hammer falls on an empty shell casing.

Shots into top of target. In pistol shooting, the shooter meets the recoil with too much heel-of-the-palm pressure, which throws the rounds high. Cure: re-wrap the pistol in your hand, and make sure to let your little finger float away from the stock.

Make sure to surprise yourself; that way you can't "push" it because you won't know when the weapon is about to fire.

Shots up and down. Could be vertical sight alignment errors, but more probably you are breathing while you shoot.

BREATHING WHILE SHOOTING DOES THIS TO YOUR TARGET. ALSO, WATCH THE TOP BLADE OF YOUR SIGHTS!

Shots off to the right. (right hander). Trigger finger too far through the guard, and you are therefore pulling the pistol to the right as you squeeze the trigger. In rifle shooting, it's called, "pulling wood."

COULD BE THAT YOUR STANCE MAKES YOU POINT RIGHT; MORE PROBIBLY, YOUR TRIGGER FINGER IS TOO FAR THRU THE GUARD, AND YOU ARE PULLING TO THE RIGHT AS YOU SQUEEZE.

24

Now that you know how to analyze shot groups made with single hand holds, you should be able to eliminate error and bring every shot under control. You can now hunt effectively, or stop a bear in his tracks in case he finds you fishing in his favorite spot.

****

But combat is different...

All my life I've played sports and seen this error: we don't practice like we play. In tennis, you see guys slug the hair off the ball in warm-up, and then dink during a match. In pistol shooting, we stand up big and tall, turn sideways, and loft a bullet delicately through the center of a paper target. But in the middle of a mild disagreement, somebody shoots at us---so we shake, rattle and roll, and wonder why we can't shoot back and hit anything.

That's why (with some exceptions) pistol instruction is terribly inadequate. We teach a method that works only for paper targets. Then we miss the real ones. Why? Because, when you're being shot at, stress, nervousness, and horrendous fear absolutely prohibit you from concentrating on any sequence of action.

Therefore, what you must have is a pistol shooting method that requires no concentration. Guaranteed, when the shooting starts, you won't be able to think. Bill Cosby's joke about his mother telling him to wear clean underwear applies. Mom: "Make sure to wear clean shorts; if you get in a car accident, you don't want the medics to find you in dirty underwear." Cosby: "So, now I bring clean shorts with me, only I don't wear them, I put them in my glove compartment."

25

In a gunfight you do the same. ..."cause when the trouble starts, first you'll say it, then you'll do it. So your shorts are going to be messy anyway..."

Also, think about this: combat shooters don't need split hair accuracy. The purpose of engaging in this sport is to stay alive, and therefore, hit the target, anywhere, anyway, anytime, often at very close range. FORGET aiming!

If you liked one hand, you will LOVE two. Two hands make you an effective combat pistol shooter. You can fire quicker and stay on target, and you can change your direction of fire rapidly and accurately. A two hand hold enables you to crouch and face your target. Therefore, any incoming rounds won't do as much damage as they would if they passed through your body sideways and destroyed two organs. Also, crouching exposes much less area than standing; thus, you reduce your chances of being hit.

LOOK! IF YOU EVEN THINK SOMEONE MIGHT SHOOT AT YOU, DRESS IN THE ULTRA-MODERN MODE. WEAR KEVLAR, AND LIVE A LITTLE LONGER...

Two-handed pistol shooting methods have been approved for a long time. Mine is different. I developed it after a lot of experimenting, and I have lots of reasons for the changes. It's faster; it exposes less body target, and I pivot quickly from the hips to line my level gun barrel up on target. In my opinion, our "PAUL" method is best, but you be the judge.

Start by using the same one handed wrap again. The point of the "V" must aim straight up your arm; if it doesn't the recoil will change your hand-hold, and your re-alignment on target won't be true again. When you have the weapon supported in a good "V" with your little finger and thumb floating free, add your other hand to the hold.

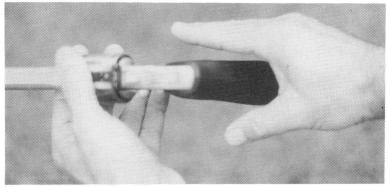

Now, interlock your left forefinger through the floating little finger of your (right) gun hand. For autoloaders, your weak hand cups to support the weapon firmly as it pulls against your gun hand.

For single and double action pistols, use the thumb of your left, (or weak) hand for cocking. This insures that your grip doesn't change during rapid fire.

Once you have the hold, you integrate it with your arms, torso and legs to build a gun platform. With both arms now extended to the weapon in front of you, and without moving the torso or pivoting the body in any way, move the weapon 15 degrees in the direction of your strong hand, (or to the right, for right-handers). By so doing, your right hand has to push slightly, and the left is forced to pull. Perfect!

Thus, you lock the weapon up with natural push/pull tension. "Natural" is the key. If you aim to the side opposite your gun hand, you have to manufacture the tension on the weapon. That's wrong. One, you won't think of it, and two, the tension will never be consistent. Also, you save time by moving into a position close to your holster. (See Hand-to-Hand Combat principles, Volume II, "get there fustus with the mostus.")

Crouch. I want your posterior as low to the ground as you can get it. If your legs are not in shape, you will have to stand a little taller and more exposed while somebody's else is trying to get you into heaven, or at least make you holey-er.

In target shooting, shaking is a no-no. In combat shooting, however, "fight or flight" response is inevitable; you'll secrete enough adrenalin to shake more than a Tahitian dancer.

That's why we use the PAUL hold. This is not for paper target shooters, but for real-life episodes; it locks the weapon in tight and allows you to pump lead into your target with precision and speed.

Your whole platform rotates for each different target, so barrel elevation doesn't change. Think, PLATFORM ACCURACY, & UNITIZED LEVEL. You use your whole body as a stable gun PLATFORM for bullet placement ACCURACY and then UNITIZE the barrel of the weapon on a constant LEVEL as you pivot from the hips. The result: Devastation. You can spin in any direction, and make any target wholly holey.

So crouch. Spread your legs wide apart, both

to the side and front.   Lead with your strong leg.
Get your belly button as low to ground as possible.
You're almost in a karate front stance,   but your
weight is EVENLY distributed, 50/50 on each leg.

Another more important reason for the PAUL
crouch is this: Performance always diminishes when
humans come under stress.   It's rather stressy when
there are no second place winners.   You would like
to stay alive, and somebody else wants to kill you.

THEREFORE, you just can't afford to use a
shooting   method   that   requires   thought   or
concentration.   Your survival mandates that EVERY
move must be done by rote.

My pastor used to preach, "you put your
raincoat on BEFORE you go out into the weather.
That's why you study the Bible BEFORE temptation
hits you. Combat pistol shooting is the same.   You
practice and determine how your life is going to
go--on or off.

This is a tough thing to tell you,   but if you
fail to decide now whether or not you want to kill
anybody,   you will hesitate and think it over when
the bullets are flying.   Hopefully,   you will have
decided to follow Christ by that time,   because
while you are trying to decide whether to kill   or
not to kill,   you will most likely meet your Maker.

About 17 years ago, a San Diego police officer
by the name of Varley and I chased burglars to a
cheap motel,   where we obtained a room key from the
manager.   On tip-toe, we climbed wooden stairs,
carefully inserted the key in the door and saw two
little juveniles (17 yrs) asleep in their beds.
Varley tiptoed in; I followed.   As he shook the
two kids awake, I heard a switch blade click in a
curtained alcove behind us, and I spun around to

29

see a third kid come out with a knife. I could not believe how fast I had my stash gun (.380 auto) trained two inches from his nose; I was a bare hair away from killing him. He froze and dropped the knife, so I eased my safety on and just stood there, shaking.

I've only been a Christian for about 5 years, so guaranteed, back then I had different attitudes. I thought I should have killed the kid and done society a favor.

Varley and I talked about it later. This was his wisdom: "Even if the little puke had stabbed me in the back and killed me, the State would not punish him with the death penalty, so why should we play God?"

I share this so you can decide now whether or not you want to kill anybody. If you do, that's between you and God. Just do this: decide now. When you're being shot at, you CAN NOT even think straight, much less make a proper decision. It always amazes me when they put police officers on trial for shooting, and try to judge him in a half-asleep courtroom. What they need to do is snarl at the jurors and shoot a few close rounds past them. Then---let'em decide.

Should you decide to lay down your life in a spirit of Christ-like sacrifice, I admire you, and you don't need to read further. On the other hand, if you plan on stopping someone who may be trying to take your life, this is how:

As you draw, POP into a PAUL stance, and even as you do this, let a round go down on the ground, somewhere midway between you and your target. I published an article about this in AMERICAN HANDGUNNER ANNUAL, but I didn't explain all of the

30

reasons why. Here---is the rest of the story.

Round nose bullets make clean and neat holes through target bodies. Clean and neat holes often don't stop the fight. But, ricochets shock, blast and maim any body in their way. Direct hits on targets with one round make one hole. Ricochets take along a lot of high-speed chips of asphalt, concrete, gravel and sand off the ground.

THE WEAPON GOES IN THE "V" OF YOUR HAND, SO RECOIL IS IN LINE WITH YOUR FOREARM.

Muzzle blast doesn't scare very many people. (If they use a gun, they're used to it.) Therefore, no fear, no adrenalin. However, ricochets tell your customer a bullet is looking for him, and he wets his pants. That's good; scared customers can't shoot back accurately at you. But a quick hit with anything, even dust, stuns and weakens your target from fear, and therefore sets him up. (That's why set-up punches are used by boxers so often.)

NOTE THE BALL PEN MARK ON MY FOREFINGER IN THIS PICTURE. THAT'S WHERE THE TRIGGER GOES, EACH AND EVERY TIME!

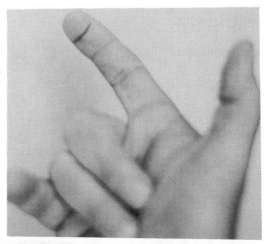

Finally, in over 50% of quick combat conflicts, the shooter misses by shooting too high. For you, putting a round-on-the-ground acts as a sighter and it tells you how high to elevate your platform in order to properly perforate the perp.

Unitized Level is obtained in much the same manner with pistols as with shotguns. You locate all the stable position points in your platform, and use these to maintain a level barrel.

If you take the time to do all this, your barrel isn't the only thing that will stay level; you'll also maintain a level head, and that's the most important thing in combat pistol shooting.

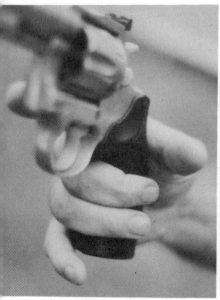

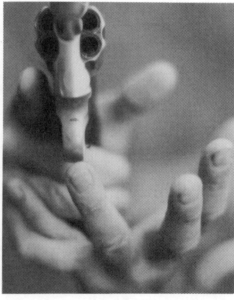

ONLY YOUR
RING FINGER +
MIDDLE FINGER
HOLD THE PISTOL.

INTERLOCK THE LITTLE FINGER OF YOUR LEFT HAND BETWEEN THE LITTLE, AND RING-FINGER OF YOUR RIGHT HAND.

Chapter 3
"Long distance, calling collect, from..."
THE ULTIMATE RIFLEMAN

Begin by understanding the function of this long gun. Used right, it will reach out hundreds of yards and destroy your target. Pistols and shotguns are no match for it unless the nut holding on to the stock decides to move into closer range.

Most pistol matches are shot at 50 ft. Shotguns might be persuaded to do business from a hundred yards. But a rifle will really reach. I have shot in lots of thousand-yard matches with metallic sights (not scopes). It's done all the time, and I am going to show you how.

To be good, learn to hold, *B-R-A-S-S, and get perfect shots off. To be excellent, however, learn to read the wind. Once the lead leaves the muzzle, the wind pretty much decides where the lead arrives.

*Breathe, Relax, Aim, Squeeeze, Surprise!

For a couple of years, I hunted with an engineer who had to prove himself. On one hunting trip, he set some cans up about 20 feet away, took careful aim through a high powered scope on his rifle, and hit it. He was elated. I laughed. He could have hit the can with a rock.

But the story illustrates how people misunderstand the nature of a rifle. It's a looong range weapon. How long depends on how tight a group you can shoot. If your 100 yd shots spray six inches all over the target, your thousand yard shots will spray 60 inches all over the landscape.

So **THE** trick in rifle shooting can be expressed in this truth:

TIGHTEN YOUR GROUP,
AND YOU LENGTHEN YOUR RANGE.

Therefore, we are going to teach you how to group tightly. Once you can do this, we'll show you how to compensate for cross winds and gravity, and still land your rounds exactly on target.

We begin by finding the weapon's zero and inherent grouping ability. In an Army class once, I took a survey; nobody understood MOA. Rifle accuracy is measured in MOA, and you adjust most sights by clicking them one MOA; that's the measurement. Thus, you need to know not only what MOA is, but how it affects bullet strike. One MOA means one Minute Of Angle, (1/60th of a degree). It's the standard for measuring bullet flight variation.

ONE DEGREE divides into sixty minutes of angle

To zero your rifle, the weapon must be motionless. With the forward part of the stock (NOT the barrel) on a sand bag, DO NOT LET THE WEAPON MOVE AS YOU SHOOT.

SHOOT FROM 100 YARDS, because it's easy and wind doesn't get a chance to move the bullet much. Aim at a precise point on the target. Very carefully, BRASS: Breathe, Relax, Aim, Squeeze, and Surprise yourself each time you let three rounds fly.

Connect the dots (bullet holes on the target) and make a triangle. From the center of that triangle, measure vertically and horizontally to your aiming point. You now have two sight changes to make.

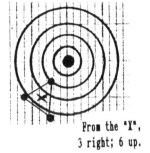

From the "Y", 3 right; 6 up.

Think: If I raise the rear sight, where will the barrel have to move as I keep the sights on target? Answer: Muzzle up. If I move my rear sight to the left, which way will the barrel have to move. Answer: muzzle left. Therefore, the rule is: the bullet striking point FOLLOWS the movement of the rear sight, and goes OPPOSITE the movement of the front sight.

You will move the strike of the bullet into the bullseye by putting on the correct MOA for both windage (side to side) and elevation (height). Suppose the center of your triangle was three inches left and five inches high from the bullseye. You move the rear sight three minutes right, and five inches low to move the strike of the bullet correspondingly. Thus adjusted, the weapon will shoot where you aim.

35

Only two forces affect the bullet after it leaves your barrel. One of those is gravity. Let me try you on a question...

DROP THIS

SHOOT THIS

Suppose you hold a rifle barrel perfectly level, and shoot across perfectly level land. At the same time you shoot one bullet out the muzzle, another bullet drops straight down. Which bullet hits the ground first?

Answer: Neither. They both land at the same time because the ONLY force that acts on them is gravity, and they drop the same distance.

Flat shooting weapons don't really shoot flat, they just speed a bullet a long distance before it gets a chance to drop to the ground.

When you shoot a rifle, you shoot the bullet upwards, and the bullet arcs towards the target like a long pass in football. The higher into the air you shoot, the longer the pass you throw.

My favorite nomographic data reference.

Most hunters I know sight their rifles in for 200 or 300 yards. That's wrong. Even if you estimate distance precisely out at 400 yards when your zero is set for 300, you will have to hold over (above) your target and block your view, so you're forced to estimate hold-over in background brush rather than target body. Finally, you have to try and dump a bullet on target like a soft ball slow pitcher.

I know a better way. Sight in at 500 yards, and memorize your bullet's mid-range trajectory. Then, at shorter range, you hold (aim) under, which means you can watch your target, estimate vertical distance accurately on the animals body, stay sighted on target if your prey moves, and make good, clean kills, instead of guessing. To accomplish all of this, we use ballistic data for your bullet and build a trajectory nomograph.

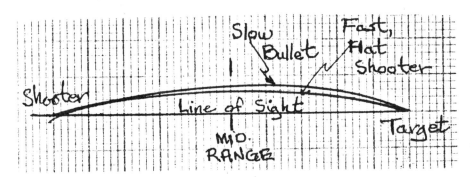

A nomograph is a, side-view diagram of trajectory that tells exactly how gravity acts on a given bullet. They are simple to make. I use graph paper and scale a straight line out to five hundred yards, which represents line of sight (aim). Above this line at two hundred and fifty yards, I measure up in inches whatever the data calls out, generally, about 10-14 inches on a moderate velocity, (2,800 fps) 150-180 grain round.

Done this way, mis-estimation of shooting range doesn't mean much, especially when you consider the damage potential of a soft nose bullet.

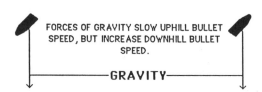

FORCES OF GRAVITY SLOW UPHILL BULLET SPEED, BUT INCREASE DOWNHILL BULLET SPEED.

———GRAVITY———

Most often, a rifle shot is taken up, or down hill. These are the forces that affect bullet flight: Gravity, drag (wind resistence) and side wind. When shooting uphill, bullets will slow down quicker due to gravity. On a downhill shot, gravity adds to bullet speed; the round does not drop so severely.

So, GO WITH THIS GENERAL RULE:
If you are shooting upwards: hold high.
If you are shooting downhill: hold low.

**Lots of rifles use a rear
leaf sight that flips up.**

**Focus on the front sight,
and the rear sight will
look a little fuzzy, like this.**

38

Theoretically, every time you line up your sights and send lead down range, the barrel should be pointing at exactly the same place. The bullet spins down the barrel at correct velocity, flies through the air, and goes through exactly the same hole it made with the last shot. But it only happens in Hollywood. In real life, the nut behind the butt plate screws up.

At Ft. Ord, I was shooting in a practice match next to an old Master-shooter by the name of Johnson. We had a new 2nd lieutenant who came down to "supervise." Johnson shot an offhand miss.

The lieutenant demanded, "Where'd that bullet land!"

Johnson turned and smiled. "Sir, it's still on its way---to Salinas."

Over a dozen good reasons exist why you can pull a trigger, and instead of scoring, send a bullet north for the summer. What could have gone wrong?

Bad stance or position ; wrong or loose sling; flinch, or hunch; wrong sight alignment or sight picture; terrible trigger control---either a jerk or a hunch because of failure to trust wobble; rounds too long in the chamber, which heat up, and then shoot hot and high; increased wobble due to nerves, breathing while shooting; wind changes or wind misread; or broken concentration. Whew!

If you take up a wrong STANCE or shooting POSITION, resulting muscle strain will unstabilize your shooting platform. Here are some bad examples:
Standing. Feet not planted to provide natural point of aim. Prone. Elbow not under the weapon.

If you are shooting from a standing position without using outside support, the weapon must be supported EQUALLY by both arms so that your hold on the rifle is balanced. Make a conscious effort to do this. The common mistake is to hold 75% of the weight with your non-trigger arm, which strains muscles and causes you to shake. You need to make sure that you AND the weapon remain motionless until the bullet leaves the barrel.

If your SLING is loose, arm support for the weapon must rely on muscle strain. Strain---and sooner or later you will get the shakes---bad for accurate bullet placement. A loop sling is best, but a hasty sling will do almost as well. Just make sure the weapon is snugly pressed into your shoulder.

As you shoot at various targets, the whole torso rotates. Of course, if your target is moving, you will follow through and continue to move with the target after the shot, just as you would with a shotgun.

From any position, try and rest the rifle on something. Super rifle shooters often cut a long stick from a tree and support their weapon as they shoot standing. Of course, don't let the barrel rest on anything; use support only on the stock.

Now, I know that a lot of shooters have invested heavily in great wood pieces and spent hours rubbing them with oil. They might flinch when they think of resting their stocks on a rock. So this is a good time to discuss rifle utility.

Customize. Pad the forearm and the pistol grip with non-slip rubber. You can use the same behind the butt plate to keep that from slipping as well. Pad your Monte Carlo cheek piece with a thin layer of foam rubber. That way, you won't be bothered by the cold against your cheek as you shoot, and your concentration will be better. Of course, recoil won't bother you as much, either.

Also, adjust the stock for length. You want the weapon to fall into shooting place, so you keep the stock as long as you would a shotgun: Measure from the trigger finger's first joint to the inside of your elbow with your arm at a ninety degree angle, and make the stock that long. In most cases, you will be adding spacers on the rifle butt.

As long as you are customizing, have your trigger worked on. A rifle with a scratchy, (NOT CRISP) trigger pull is a great hindrance to accurate shooting. While you are having the trigger stoned for crispness, adjust its pull weight. Most gunsmiths like 7 pounds of pull, I like four (almost a hair trigger).

Finally, do something with those sights! Most sighting systems on rifles are really poor. You need a set of sights that will perform in semi-darkness, at least. Improve sight visibility with fluorescent paint, and perhaps change over to a sighting system that will adjust so you can fine-tune your weapon's zero.

From sitting or prone positions, rests are easier to use. Given enough time and a defensive position, such as your home, you can fill a pillowcase or bag with sand. Laying a weapon's stock across one of these will settle your wobble down enough to increase your effective range by a couple of hundred yards, or more.

Although a rifle's longer sight base is more forgiving, SIGHT ALIGNMENT errors are still the kiss-of-death for accurate bullet placement. The key here is consistency. You may not align the correct way, but if your alignment is the same every time, you can be a precision shooter.

SIGHT PICTURE in rifle shooting is important, and we obtain it by placing ALIGNED SIGHTS in proper relation to the target. Pistols shoot from close range, so you don't have to look at the target; instead you stare at your sights. In rifle shooting, we look at the target, and make sure the point of aim is correct. So, the focus of the eye is critical and it goes:

FROM:

REAR SIGHT, to
FRONT SIGHT, to
TARGET, then back to
FRONT SIGHT again.

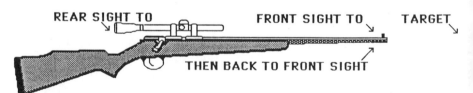

EYE FOCUS SEQUENCE IS ONLY FOR METALIC SIGHTS.
WITH A SCOPE, JUST PUT THE RETICLE ON TARGET AND SQUEEZE

If you are not surprised when the weapon fires, you will probably FLINCH OR HUNCH. (I've seen pros slap their trigger, hunch, and dump rounds into the target butts.) You will stand there and begin to wobble, so you squeeze too fast, and anticipate recoil by hunching your shoulder forward. A different body reaction to the same kind of anticipation is flinching, in which you merely tighten up and disturb sight alignment. If you don't squeeze gently, straight-to-the-rear, with a smooth increase in pressure, your failure in trigger control will <u>disturb</u> <u>sight</u> <u>alignment</u>, and you will spray bullets all over the landscape.

What's the cure? A coach pretends to load the weapon for the shooter. (But really, he leaves it empty.) Then, the shooter jerks as the trigger clicks. Repetitive dry firing corrects the problem. In the pistol section we learned: ALIGN THE SIGHTS ON TARGET, AND CAUSE THE HAMMER TO FALL WITHOUT DISTURBING THE SIGHTS. That's the key, and dry firing makes it automatic.

You know what separates the men from the boys in rifle shooting? WIND! Anytime you send a round two or three hundred yards away from you, the wind will move it around enough to matter. I've shot in matches where the wind has moved the strike of my bullet twenty three inches! Wind is even more bothersome to a lighter bullet; a slight 5 mph breeze makes a difference, especially a crosswind.

RUGER MINI-14

MINE IS STAINLESS. GREAT GUN, AS RUGERS ARE, BUT .223'S ARE LIKE FEATHERS IN THE WIND.

So, to be a good long range shot with a rifle, you have to read the wind. Pay close attention to your environment. See how the trees, grass, or bushes are being blown. Take special note of how the wind blows in relation to your bullet's flight.

You can learn to read wind to a fine fair hair with a 20 power shooting scope. It tells you exactly what the wind is doing. Pay attention while you are shooting. If the wind changes while you are preparing to shoot, adjust. If you know the wind is pushing your bullets to the right, adjust your rear sight to the left. The trick-of-the-trade is: How much?

Feel it. Look at the trees to see where the wind is coming from, and learn to feel how strong it is. Then, use Kentucky windage---hold, and aim off towards the windy side. Short range shots require less adjustment because the bullet arrives so quickly that the wind vector doesn't have time to act on it.

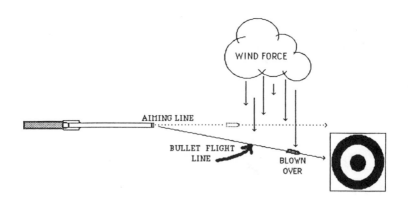

Focus on target, then change the focus short. That's SHORT! Focus on something halfway between you and your target.

Focus long by mistake and you will read the wind BACKWARDS!

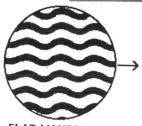

FLAT WAVES COME FROM FASTER WIND

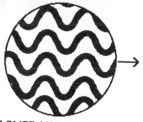

SLOWER WIND PRODUCES TALLER HEAT WAVES

Look at the heat waves drifting across the lens. If the waves are big, the wind is not blowing much. If they are flattened out and moving fast, your bullet has much more to contend with.

WHEN HEAT WAVES GO STRAIGHT UP

YOU ARE LOOKING INTO THE WIND

Now, turn the scope in to the wind. When the heat waves move straight up, (a boil) you are looking directly into it. The direction of the wind in relation to bullet path tells you the force value of the wind vector. If it comes in from a 45 degree angle, it will be worth about half, so put on half the windage you normally would. Wind directly from the side will make the bullet's push come to shove. Adjust for it, big time.

With the knowledge you now have, you should be able to control your weapon so well that it is motionless as the round leaves the barrel. After that, gravity and wind have been compensated for. The result: Precision accuracy--from a long distance away.

Finally, we talk about training.

PRACTICE THE SAME WAY YOU WILL SHOOT.

(In GREAT LIVIN' IN GRUBBY TIMES, Book II of this series, we teach the following in much greater detail.)

Popping rounds at paper by yourself during the day may be enjoyable, but it has nothing to do with night shooting on a team. Think about the reality of a survival situation and practice for it. Never think of yourselves as individual shooters; know that you are part of a team, and work that way.

If you don't practice the way you will shoot, a firing opportunity will arise, and this will happen: The whole team will blast away as if it is the beginning of World War III. And then---it will be quiet all of a sudden, while everybody sits around and reloads. In other words, your team will suffer extended down time, when not one person has any ammo in a weapon. Trouble.

Use your best terrain analyst as fire direction control leader, not your best shooter. Position your team members so that you can shoot into your whole surrounding area with effective fire. Practice going into position on signal (whistle or hand signal) and then talk to each other about your fields of fire, making sure that each shooter has a slight firing overlap.

Be quiet while moving into firing position, but once a cap is busted, the noise doesn't matter. Talk to each other. Chatter. Keep everyone informed, and learn to listen. If you know where your team members are, or what they are doing, you can coordinate your effort, and you become highly effective.

Move fast. Your primary function is to keep your team safe. You are not shooting film--you want zero exposure. Don't take risks. Above all, don't let anyone get hit. If you think exposure is worth it, suture self...

Successful survival shooting must be a team effort. You will work as a team in other endeavors, and shooting is no exception.

Practice as a team the way you will work, and you will enhance your ability many times over. Then, when it comes to shooting, you can be the best there is.

GETTING DOWN.
If someone yells, "GET DOWN!"
and you think that means
stand up and be-bop, make out a will
and stay close to God.

Section II

THE GREEN BERETS' TEAM METHODS.

Applying the Principles

BEST SURVIVAL BET
THE GREEN BERET TEAM CONCEPT

Scene: American Revolution begins. George Washington writes, "We either hang together, or we hang--separately."

If you want to survive, hang (in there) together. To be succesful, CHOOSE a few good people, bring them TOGETHER, have each member SPECIALIZE, then practice and train tough together.

A quantity of people doesn't mean much in a survival situation. In fact, a multitude will multiply your problems. But if your people are trained and dedicated, you have power. Whether it's construction or destruction, defense or offense, you can accomplish a lot more.

If you had to do it alone, how long would it take you to build a bicycle? Wouldn't your task by much easier if specialists made wheels, frame, pedals and brakes? Likewise with survival functions----a joint effort pays off tremendously.

One of the reasons togetherness pays off so well is called "group dynamics." When two or more humans work together, one person will energize the other with an idea or effort that never would have been possible had either been working alone.

Economic factors also help when teaming up. Two can live cheaper than one, and a community of dedicated individuals, with decent leadership, can enjoy fantastic economic benefits.

For example, our team uses a central shop. We all contributed to the tool fund, and we have everything we need at a fraction of the cost. Several of us live on one parcel of land, so we save the expense of separate plots. We grow food in common, and our livestock is shared. We own common vehicles, such as a flatbed truck. Living this way is cheap and easier if you are all pulling in the same direction. Otherwise, you won't have much more than a U.S. Congress.

A team with a common cause works. Some examples: The Israelis---religiously motivated to do the very best in training, and almost unbeatable in war. The Ghurkas---for whom return home from the British Army without an honorable discharge makes one a social outcast.

A contra-example: The U.S. population during Vietnam. The draft dodgers moved to Canada. The rest fought and died. The divisiveness in our military ranks was portrayed in the movie, PLATOON.

Find dedicated people; they will train hard, share well, endure without complaint, and work TOGETHER; they will be winners. Fail---and you wind up with a disjointed group of individuals, who sing their own national anthem:
"Oh say can you see, what is in it for me?"

Chapter 4

HOW TO CHOOSE TEAM MEMBERS

During the month of June in California, our Special Forces Team was ordered to take one hundred National Guardsmen to the Colorado River and teach them how to use rubber boats. Then we paddled with them down river to a pickup point.

It should have been a pleasant weekend, but it turned into a rout---and near disaster.

Before the story, look at the respective attitudes:

SPECIAL FORCES TEAM	NATIONAL GUARD COMPANY
Dedicated to team first	Interested in self only
Goal to accomplish	Aimless
Trying hard to learn	Didn't care to know
Practice, long and hard	Play it cool, drink beer
Willpower, self control	Lay around, do what feels good

After they became tired, they wouldn't paddle. We had to make camp. They had ditched survival gear to make room for beer, and when the mosquitoes and rain attacked, they had no netting. Some actually broke down and cried. One boat mutinied. They argued about which way to go, and the argument developed into a fight. Pride was everywhere. They broke into factions, and switched loyalties repeatedly. In the end, they defeated themselves before they had a chance to win. Even with a strength of over fifty men, they were useless.

Maybe today, however, things have improved. My experience happened during Vietnam days, and the Guard Units attracted draft dodgers. What the story proves, however, is this: It's quality, not quantity that counts. In order to obtain quality, you have to start with character, because knowledge and ability are nothing without it.

I used to know a very talented neuro-surgeon who was also an alcoholic. At times he was brilliant, and you might have thought he would be a great team member. But survival occurs when the going gets tough---and the tough get going. Not for him...When his going got tough, his bottle got going.

As Bill Gothard says in his BASIC YOUTH CONFLICTS seminars, "Success at anything requires 95% character and 5% ability." That's because you can teach a person with character almost anything. On the other hand, ability without character will be worthless in a tight pinch, because people of weak character leave you hanging, frequently when you need them most. Thus, in order to make a good team, you need men and women of principle and character.

It goes like this: If a man tries to build himself up with outside support, it never works, and he lives unsatisfied. Scripture says, "For whoever wants to save his life will lose it, but whoever loses his life for me and for the Gospel, will save it." If God controls your life, you have nothing to prove. Otherwise---struggle by yourself.

Pride is the root sin which causes men to use a variety of outside escapes or boosters, none of which work. Alcohol, drugs, multiple female relationships all go to boost the man, but in reality, they tear him down. So a person who constantly builds himself up is always lacking, and thus re-inforces the need to build himself up more.

People who are addicted to drugs, alcohol or casual sex might as well wear a chain around their neck. The chain comes first; it's the center of their lives, and their need will always be far above the needs of other team members. You cannot use a "me-first" person; you have no hope of counting on them when things get tough. Dedicated lechers are likewise weak choices for team membership. When a person spends all of his time thinking, talking and dreaming about his next conquest, he has very little real time to dedicate to team interest. Find pride in a potential team member, and you've discovered a loser.

What you need is a person who successfully places himself in a subordinate position to others. He is thoughtful, kind, and courteous. On the other hand, listen to what Paul wrote about bad choices for team membership in Galations 5:19. "...hatred, discord, jealousy, selfish ambitions, dessensions, factions, envy, and the like..." If your new applicant exhibits any of these attributes, get rid of him.

53

Pride will show in one of three ways: a temporal value system, moral impurity, or bitterness. Any of these attributes found in a prospective team member mean trouble.

Also, be careful with people who have a welfare state of mind. Easy money schemes, actual welfare receipts in personal history, something for nothing taken and bragged about---these, and anything even like these, and that person is OUT. They are worthless for a team effort. Worse, they lie; you can't get a straight answer from them, so you never know where you are.

Often, poor character traits don't show up during an interview. The best in appearance is frequently the worst in practice. Why? Humans often compensate for a negative self image by putting up a terrific front. If you don't believe me, get to know some of the beauties from the singles' bars.

But heart attitudes and thoughts control words and actions, so sooner or later, the truth will out. Therefore, it's best to take all new team members on a probation basis, say six months.

On the positive side, you're looking for a person who is faithful, in these ways:

FAITHFUL without recognition. You want a person who is motivated to do things because they are simply the right things to do. Watch out for grand-standers. The drive to get recognition surpasses human ability to satisfy it, and therefore leads to a 3-D condition:

Disappointment,
Dissatisfaction, and then,
Discord, after which everybody suffers.

The best test is faithfulness, or fidelity. Apparantly, that's what the Marine Corps thinks also; their motto is Semper Fidelis, (Semper Fi) which means, "Always Faithful."

FAITHFUL in the dark alone means he will perform with a dedicated heart when nobody is watching him.

FAITHFUL with a little means you can tell if a person will be faithful with a lot; just try him with a small amount.

FAITHFUL with another's..., which includes a reputation. People not faithful with another's reputation (gossip prone) are frequently untrustworthy with others' possessions or money.

As mentioned before, your team needs to work as one unit. Survival is just going to be easiest if you don't start off with arguments arising out of deep differences in belief. Spiritual unity is best. If you're Jewish, go with that. Catholic, the same. Christians are great for me because I can call them to Scripture to settle conflicts.

I believe also that ethnic solidarity is best. Intra-team prejudice is absolutely counter-productive to success at pulling together as an effective team.

Psychological compatibility hasn't shown me much. People of good character adjust to each other, but similar personalities often produce tremendous friction.

I like the intelligence measure, as does Army Special Forces. That's because it takes a degree of character to suffer the inconvenience of obtaining an education. Brains and muscles are similar. Work them out a little, and their capacities increase.

Don't for a minute think that all your team members have to be young. Older people are excellent choices for two reasons: A. they are frequently knowledgeable and wise, and B. they grew up at a time when the world was not so far removed from good christian ethics, so their character was formed and enhanced with wisdom and proper attitudes. In old folks, I find wisdom, and quite a bit of shrewdness.

Finally, take a look at health records. See if muscle development is missing. A surf 'n sand physique won't do, (two arms, two legs and a beach ball), because excessive fat tissue is a sign of weak character. Uncontrolled appetite, need to gratify self in disregard of health, (tobacco), and lack of proper exercise mean that this person could easily fail you when times get tough.

I like a physical fitness test in addition. Are the legs strong? Can this person perform sustained, strong, physical labor? An average measure would call for five chinups, 20 pushups, 30 sit-ups, and running for a mile in under eight minutes. People who can sustain a high level of physical output show me that they put their bodies to a bit of pain and improved. That shows character.

If you can find a few good members for your survival team, you are off to a great start, because it only takes a small nucleus of quality people to form an invincible unit.

On the other hand, one bad apple...

POLISH YOUR
KNIFE; THEN
USE IT FOR
EMERGENCIES
AS A SIGNAL
DEVICE.

EVERYBODY'S
KNIFE
BIBLE

Chapter 5

BUILDING TEAM UNITY
CONFERENCE PLANNING

For a new baby, the most important thing is growth. It needs to be taught, trained, and tested. Gradually it adjusts to its environment and begins responding to the demands of the world around it.

Your new team is your baby. It also needs to grow, and therefore requires teaching, training and testing before it adjusts and responds to demand. But the team will have one problem that a newborn baby doesn't: it will need to learn how to work as one body.

You begin working on that problem the moment you form the team, and you never stop. If team members don't adjust to one another, your team will function like a human body with a rejected heart transplant.

The troublesome nature of working human relationships was defined almost two thousand years ago by St. Paul when he wrote in I Corinthians, 7:28, ..."they will have trouble in this life." There, he was talking about married couples who enjoy a natural and mutual physical release that helps keep peace in the family. Your team members don't have that option.

Just look around and notice---all the things we have on earth are in short supply, be they time, food, ammunition or attention. Once you have a group of self centered humans competing for these things, conflict is sure to arise. Adjustment is often difficult, and biased opinions frequently grow into a contest of wills, which then become personality conflicts.

As in medicine, the key is catching the disease in its early stages. Late stages of personality conflicts often become raging fights, and the wedges driven into the relationship stay embedded there for long, painful years.

What's the result? Instead of harmony and shared work toward common goals, individual egos interfere with teamwork. If you want to see a living, ~~working~~ example, watch our Congress.

You need to know this: Adjust is an intransitive verb. You don't adjust somebody else. See, no matter how wrong the other person was, no matter what happened, you can't make the other guy change, it is **you** who must do the adjusting. Easier said than done...it requires humility at best and a respectable self image at least. (Will Rogers said, "You can always tell the size of a man by the size of the thing that makes him mad.") Neither persuasion, argument, threats, or force

will do it, because, "a man convinced against his
will, is of the same opinion still."

If an offended team member can not forgive
and forget, he must at least be able to place the
team health before his own self interest, and lump
it. That's a very difficult thing to do; and that
is why we teach you that GOOD CHARACTER is the main
ingredient you look for when choosing a team
member.

SOLVING HUMAN CONFLICT

If finger prints, ear prints and teeth
are all different, so are people. Christian
pastors teach that gaps between human beings are
inevitable. We are free willed beings, all
different; we have different drives, opinions,
reactions, and emotions. The differences create
conflicts--how severe depends on the desperation of
the individuals who happen to be opposed to one
another.

In conflict, two opposing parties can
choose one of five solutions:

WIN
WITHDRAW
LOSE
COMPROMISE
RESOLVE

Winning is frequently a compulsion that
compensates for a negative self image. If you, or
the person you are in controversy with MUST win,
that's trouble, because humans use sarcasm, name-
calling, personal insults, and physical combat. If
both MUST win, much bigger trouble is on the
horizon, because two winners opposed to each other
cannot co-exist in peace.

Only war will enable one of them to prevail. (see James 4:1) "What causes fights and quarrels among you? Don't they come from your desires that battle within you?

OFFENSES BETWEEN HUMANS ARE PRECISELY MEASUREABLE.

To determine the true degree of offense, **ADD** the insensitivity of the offending jerk to the sensitivity of the victim. In mathematical terms:

STRIKE + SENSITIVITY TO PAIN = INJURY

Some problems might be solved by directing behavioral modification in a member, but doing so is an <u>exclusive</u> function of leadership. Again, a good rule to follow in making corrections is found in Galations 6:1, which says, "...restore him gently. But watch yourself, or you also may be tempted."

Any other team member "correcting" a fellow member will probably create more heat than light. Even when a leader corrects, he does so gently; otherwise he brings about the first stage of abnormal social development by wounding a team member's spirit. (Gothard, Basic Youth Conflicts Seminar)

When accused, disapproved of, or chastised, the drive for self preservation compels a person to attack in self defense or withdraw.

THE SEVERITY OF THE COMPULSION TO WIN, GET UP–AND–OVER, OR CONQUER, IS CREATED BY THE LACK OF SELF IMAGE IN THE BAD ACTOR.

The chaplain is the person who can nip most of these problems in the bud; he reports to the team leader. As often as the team leader sees the need, the team should be called together and relationships should be worked on.

If offended, write a note; try and be the first to apologize.

I've found that, Christian or not, the rules laid out in the Bible provide a fine rule for members of any society to use in promoting harmony. For example, the Bible forbids backbiting and gossip, something that destroys team unity.

Therefore, another hard and fast rule is: nobody is allowed to bad mouth another team member, nor is anyone allowed to hear a bad report about another. Hawaii was first a deeply christian State, and today, the expression still holds: "Eh brah; no talk stink!" That cuts down on a lot of griping, thus helping to maintain a cheerful atmosphere.

Finally, no one person is allowed to join, even in attitude, with another against team policy, a personal injury, or any grievance. It's called "taking up an offense." St Paul called it, "factions." Within the team, one person's misunderstandings and complaints stay one's own.

It would appear that the above rules were developed by common sense, but they all are found in the Manufacturer's Handbook for Humanity, the Bible. If you fail to love your (team) neighbors, you will suffer many of the fruits of the flesh found in Galatians 5:19.

If you have lived long enough to read this book, attended school or seen a broken home, you will recognize some of the symptoms St Paul wrote about: "The acts of the sinful nature are obvious, sexual immorality, discord, hatred, impurity and debauchery...jealousy, fits of rage, selfish ambition, dissensions, factions and envy, drunkenness..."

See? It's like a final exam for human compatability.

If I had to choose any group to survive with, I guarantee you, it would NOT be a Galatian Those kinds of trouble will kill your team. Why? Because "a house divided against itself cannot stand."

But once you have your team in harmony, you're ready to make great progress. Every positive step you take will produce great results.

PARTY A ——— PARTY B

**GRADES IN
CONFLICT
A= PASS
F= FLUNK**

62

Communicate! That's how you work together. Here, I communicate without saying a word. If you don't have radios and you are too far apart to shout, send code. A cheap signal mirror let's your fingers do the walking.

If you don't want anyone else to read your mail, aim a cardboard shadow box towards your message target. The side walls of your improvised shadow box restrict the sun-flash messages to a specific area.

Chapter 6
SKILLS AND FUNCTIONS FOR INDIVIDUAL TEAM MEMBERS

Special Forces Teams function first in isolation---brief and briefback; then, they operate. Isolation occurs before any mission. The team meets, and begins to examine the problem. Each specialist studies in his own field, then makes decisions and plans for "his part in the movie."

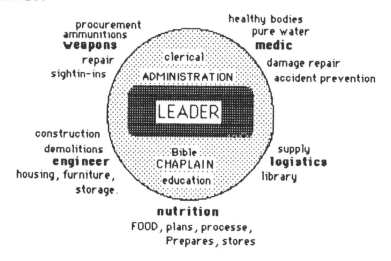

procurement
ammunitions
weapons
repair
sightin-ins

healthy bodies
pure water
medic
damage repair
accident prevention

clerical
ADMINISTRATION

LEADER

construction
demolitions
engineer
housing, furniture,
storage.

Bible
CHAPLAIN
education

supply
logistics
library

nutrition
FOOD, plans, processe,
Prepares, stores

He then relates all his relevant knowledge to the other team members in a briefback. Only after each team member has precisely planned his part, and the whole team understands the mission from each individual's standpoint, then, and then only, does the mission get off the ground.

So, your radio operator tells you his plans for contact times, frequencies, code systems, antennas to use, etc. The weapons guy explains what spare parts will be available and how firepower will be distributed. The engineer will talk about construction and demolition, tools, explosives, camouflage and concealment.

I always listened closely to the medic. He would tell us about indigenous diseases, and hazards to health, such as snakes. On one occasion, Woodcroft mentioned that a particular snake's bite was quickly fatal. But he showed us how we could save our lives. How...?

"Hold the joint of your bitten finger over the muzzle of a pistol so that it blows off cleanly when the trigger is pulled." As in this picture, you'd feel sad too if you had to kiss your finger goodbye...

As operations begin, we have frequent meetings, both formal and informal, to discuss progress, explore possibilities, and plan future moves. If goals are not met, we have plenty of lead time to correct a potentially troublesome problem. Things go smoother that way.

Needless to say, survival can be made much easier if your team operates in similar fashion. The methods are superb even though not all of the functions will apply. Certainly you won't be doing much with air drops. Likewise, you should add some team members to fill categories the military doesn't have.

Here are some of the categories in which a survival team should function:

> Team Leader
> Nutritionist
> Medic
> Weapon and hunting specialist
> Engineer
> Computronics Technologist
> Supply and logistics
> Technologist
> Chaplain

The TEAM LEADER should be finest quality. Character here is of utmost importance. In the face of life and death circumstance, he HAS to have the moral integrity to do what's right. He should be an emulatable leader. His functions are co-ordination and administration of the survival team's activities and plans. He evaluates incoming data and intelligence of all kinds, and directs appropriate response activities. He functions as judge and arbitrator, settling disputes between members. On a small team, or perhaps on a poor one, he acts as treasurer, and disperses funds to other department heads. Quite frequently he is also responsible for civil affairs, that is, speaking and dealing with outside governments or groups with whom the team deals as a whole.

A NUTRITIONIST trains in horticulture, and knows how to grow things all year round, in all kinds of containers. He can keep you alive and well because he can grow bean or alfalfa sprouts out of your backpack. It is he who understands and knows about how all wild plants can be used for food and medicine. He's a great trapper. In easier times, he sets up major butcher operations, and cures and preserves not only meats, but fruits and vegetables as well. All food supplies are his responsibility, both quantity and quality. He looks after the diet and weight, (over and under), of the whole team and reports to the team leader.

It makes things a lot nicer in a war if you know that you can sustain just about any injury and live through it. So MEDICS are a big morale factor. Emergency Medical Training (EMT) is available almost everywhere today. In addition, your team medic should know a lot about dentistry, and perform dental checks on the whole team regularly. An ounce of prevention is worth a mouthful of cure.

He is also responsible for the whole team's health and sanitation, so he checks the latrines, and monitors the purity of the water supply. Before moving the team anywhere, the medic will study the area's health problems, both indigenous disease and hazards. Then, his medical briefback informs everyone.

WEAPONS AND HUNTING. In Book II of this series, called, GREAT LIVIN' IN GRUBBY TIMES we teach survival weapon choice and combat gunnery.

Your specialist provides weaponry in all three categories. He will maintain common weapons, and co-ordinate individual acquisitions so that firepower is properly mixed and matched. (Again, see Book II, Combat Gunnery.) He recommends best weapons for particular uses. He studies land areas to make hunts meat productive. He gunsmiths, reloads, and probably is the team's best shot.

ENGINEERS speak fluent mathematics, and should know how to build or demolish anything. They would build housing, storage for food and animal feed, outbuildings for animals, fences, roads, and drainages. They should be able to plumb and electrify any structure. They do concrete work--design, forming, pouring and stripping. They can run and repair all kinds of machinery, (backhoes, trucks, etc), and understand mechanical advantages obtained from ropes, levers, and pulleys. Although demolition is a warrior's skill, it's convenient if you have an engineer who can use chicken manure, diesel fuel, and a small kicker to blast a hole anywhere.

COMPUTRONICS TECHNOLOGIST describes the team member most familiar with computers and other electronic devices. A computer is used to publish newsletters, issue plans, keep track of records, and do any kind of survival accounting. Perhaps most important is its ability to communicate with other machines, so that research is accomplished from the team's computer keyboard.

LOGISTICIANS normally handle transport and supply. Ours keeps track of all material by indexing everything on a rolodex. Carpenter's tools are indexed on blue cards, electrician's on green, and these supplies and tools are stored in one area, (on peg board painted blue or green). Everything goes back in it's place, and he spends time making sure everything is ready to perform perfectly. He sharpens, de-rusts, cleans and paints. He procures constantly, because he receives and accounts for a constant flow of funds. Our horses, canoes, boats and cars are his responsibility. He keeps track of all maintenance and always knows what needs to be done.

A TECHNOLOGIST keeps current with new developments, and will know solutions for a lot of problems when libraries and other information centers cease to function. He will be the librarian for all team reference books, most of which he reads. He constantly learns how to adapt new technology to the survival team's needs. For example, he might be the radio operator and understand the latest solar technology. Wind and hydro-electric power are his responsibility. He draws plans and works up a materials lists for new construction projects.

In my opinion, a CHAPLAIN is the most important person a team can have. He performs religious services, of course, but more than that, sees that all team members are growing in character. His job is morale, and he works at it constantly, bringing needs of individual members to the attention of the leadership, and being available to all for counsel and guidance. It's a critical job; one bad morale problem can grow like a cancer---out of control, and devastate the whole team.

Naturally, the functions and skills listed above don't have to fall into the same categories. You may have a logistician who shoots best, an engineer who sends code, or a medic with a degree in finance. In these cases, the functions switch.

As your survival team grows and you begin to accomplish goals, new needs will arise, and the team leader will have to assign additional duties. Such new needs might include projects to produce common funds, or intelligence analyst, (gathers information about the outside world and relates it to team efforts and security), animal control and training, (responsible for watchdogs and animal policy), and firefighters.

Another phenomenon occurs as the team grows and establishes itself---one team member will find himself overloaded, and therefore have to dump an area of responsibility. In such an event, somebody with a lighter load takes over.

Especially in the beginning stages, the whole team meets frequently, with the leader(s) presiding. The meeting might go like this:

Chaplain opens with prayer, then turns it over to the leader.

Leader briefs financial situation, and relates all areas of progress to projections. Then calls for reports.

Nutritionist: "We spent 87 dollars for rabbit cages. The tech's input on the water feeders worked well and we have changed over to a better system. We have team food to last 82 days at approx 1400 calories per day/per man. We are short of vitamins and iron, but the iron problem will be solved with rabbit livers. From the coming hunting season I will need 600 pounds of boned meat out of deer, bear or elk, which translates to eight hunting tags with 50% success ratio. Blackberries will be pickable in twenty days, and I need a volunteer to chaperon the kids. I have freezer room for twenty quarts. Tomatoes are coming in,

69

and should be canned next week. I expect to have two cans per man per month through the winter."

Medic: "We now have a full set of splints and enough first aid equipment for any major injury. I have a blood pressure gauge and I can teach anybody to use it. Our water system needs a new filter this month, and the water well cover should be replaced. Somebody left a bar of soap in the swim hole, and that's a no-no because it ruins the water the cows drink. Two people caught colds this month, and I have them wearing surgical masks to keep the germs from spreading."

Weapons: "We'll have good elk hunting on the lower meadows by Lobster Creek. I plan on using all the kids and driving them up this draw, (points to map). All the .308 shells are reloaded for the hunt with 165 grain hollow point boat tails coming out of the muzzle at 2600 feet per second. There is no open country, so we'll all be shooting short range. At a three hundred yard zero, your mid-range rise is five and a half inches. I have range practice with these rounds scheduled next Saturday morning for all shooters. We have 600 rounds of double ought buck for the twelve gauges, two hundred of which are available for practice. I have John's new scope mounted and bore sighted. I need three children to help cast pistol bullets for two hours. Our pistol scores are coming up, but we still need offhand work at fifty yards to get 75% hits."

Engineer: "The harvest kitchen roof is sheeted, as you all know, but I can't start shingling until I have seven more squares of handsplit shakes. I have the cedar bolts cut and on site, and the froes are sharp; it should take eight man hours to split them out. We are short of staples for the shingle gun. We are ahead of

70

schedule with that project, however, so funding isn't urgent. The canning stoves are in, and the firewood is dry. We should probably drop rock on our driveway before winter rains. I'll get with the medic and take care of the water system. I'll have two hours of backhoe time available if nutrition wants more rabbit manure on the garden. Finally, I will need help mixing cement and pouring concrete for the smokehouse foundation."

Computronics tech: "I researched 1,000 magazines and sifted 2.38 million paragraphs to learn that wind power will work for us. Also, I have repaired the short wave radio, and a new antenna gives us a lot better radio range."

Logistician: "All vehicles are in good shape. We'll need tires for the four wheel truck in about two months. I have a new system for old saw blades. If you change, and the blade you take off is not dull, it goes on the peg marked suspension so I can touch it up. The hardwood 2x6 is almost dry enough to use. We have 200 board feet available. I need six tons of hay for the cows this winter. Then I need goat feed, and the next tools should be half inch drive sockets for the air wrench. If you will set aside twenty five dollars, I'll watch the ads for a good used set."

Technologist: "The solar panels are ready for the harvest kitchen roof. I bought five new books at the used bookstore, two about wood working, one on sauna baths, a garden build-it book, and one on bicycle power. They are ready to be checked out. I am working on the plans for the underground root cellar, and I could use the backhoe for one of the free hours to cut into the ground. If I could get the engineer to mix some more cement, I could cut the log ends and have the walls in before the rains come. Incidentally, we monitored the scanner and the sheriff raided the ranch six miles east. Big marijuana crop. Our northern neighbors are in the same business. Anybody hunting over that way should be careful."

Chaplain: I am getting two hundred dollars for recreation equipment. I plan on a used ping pong table for the barn, which we can use after we get the first hay out, and we should add some weights in the exercise room. Basic Youth Conflicts is coming to Eugene and we can fill four seats on the bus. If nobody volunteers, I'll chaperon our kids at the square dance next week. There's a marriage encounter group meeting next month, and I've made two reservations. I'll contact the ones I think should go in order of priority."

The leader moderates all of the above, allowing all to speak for the time allotted. You get your message across, or let it pass. If you can't reach a decision in the time allotted, drop the subject and move on.

All for one, and one for all. Sound familiar? Each member is obliged to spend a certain amount of time for team community service, and he keeps an accurate record, on his honor. You don't have to be superhuman, but you do have to give it your best. The rest of the time is yours, and can be bartered out, or used for your own growth and progress.

As soon as team individuals have achieved proficiency in their own skills, your team is ready to start meeting on a regular basis, and the information exchanged at the meetings will really get your team growing fast.

72

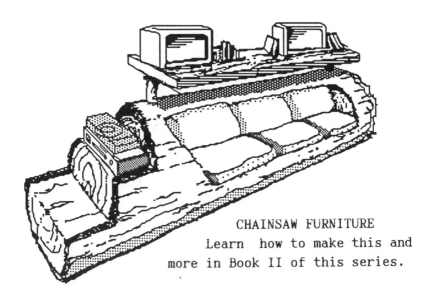

CHAINSAW FURNITURE
Learn how to make this and
more in Book II of this series.

Chapter 7

TRAINING THE TEAM

Nobody stands still in a learning curve.
They either learn more, or forget more. It's
pretty much that way with anything you learn. You
either get better, or get worse.

But you need to constantly improve.
Gothard (Basic Youth Conflicts Seminar) defines
success NOT as what you have done, but what you
have done compared to what you COULD HAVE DONE.
You need not only be as fully skilled and educated
as you can be, but moving forward in proficiency.
It's a great morale builder---for the whole team.

Teaching pre-supposes that somebody knows.
If nobody on your team knows anything about a
certain subject or skill, you will either have to
hire a teacher, or procure learning materials.

In Book II of this series, GREAT LIVIN' IN GRUBBY TIMES, we specialize in teaching individual outdoor skills, and we included enough illustrations to make the material easy to learn. With some student diligence and practice, and you should be well on your way.

Especially in the beginning, the team leader needs to assign various skills for each team member to learn. That way, you don't overlap in any specialty, and the team becomes more proficient as a whole. Then, later on, cross training (one member learns another's skill) is easier because someone else already knows, and you can get coaching.

Each member needs to set weekly goals for learning a subject. (monthly goals create temptations to wait and cram), If the goals need to be re-adjusted, the team leader should be informed.

Remember when setting study goals that you will also need time--for working together, (vital for team inter-adjustment), for growing in character, (Bible reading, chaplain counsel) for exercise, (to maintain health) and for attending planning and briefback meetings.

You need to acquire both common and specific---knowledge and skills. Bare knowledge requires no manual dexterity or physical ability; you merely know in your head---the trajectory of weapons, the pressure of water, or the calories in food. Skills require that you not only know, but can apply what you know to a situation, such as first aid, hand-to-hand combat, or land navigation.

Then, survival skills and knowledge are either common, (for the whole team), or individual (for one specialist). Common skills include: hand to hand combat, land navigation, terrain analysis, and travel methods, (canoe, horse, etc). Specific knowledge is either hi-tech or requires so much in-depth study that one team member specializes.

For example, all members should know first aid, but the medic is practically a doctor. Everyone should shoot, but the weapons specialist can draw nomographs for any powder load and bullet weight, and modify most firearms. The whole team should be aware of the principles of camouflage and noise discipline, but the engineer is responsible for cover and concealment. When your team trains, both individual and team skills are polished.

Incidentally, only one person needs to train animals, but every team member should be familiar with them, especially the attack dogs.

Some of the members who undergo complicated learning tasks need extra time. If everybody is shoveling out an underground root cellar, but the medic needs to learn broken bone treatment, let him study. The limb you save might be your own.

Since all team members should stay physically fit, every training session should include physical exercise, led by the specialist assigned in that area. If some of your team members are older folks, they get special exercise, and the medic will check pulses. By making sure to do this, everybody will be physically prepared.

I also recommend that every training time include character development by the team chaplain. It's most important. "Knowledge without character is like power without restraint." (Pastor D Church)

Many of us are confused about God, especially after the Jim and Tammy Bakker show. But a writer isn't worth much if he doesn't impart sense to his subject matter. Nobody is telling you to believe in God, but my experience proves this: There are natural laws on the earth, such as, water freezes at 32 degrees; things fall down; not up.

I suspect that the same author of the physical laws (which are always true and never change) also figured out and wrote the spiritual laws. Therefore, it just might be that Scripture also never fails to work. I am pretty sure that whether we choose to believe or not doesn't much matter. The laws always operate, and just like water freezing and apples falling down, our personal beliefs have no influence. Just as they are set in Nature, and they are set in Scripture.

If you want your team to survive, it's a good idea to be physically strong, mentally bright, and spiritually sound. Ignoring that last vital part of the complete man could very well be your undoing... So, grow spiritually. Make it a part of every training session.

Common work projects during training time are a great idea. It gives the team a spirit of camaraderie and accomplishment, thereby building morale. Lots of tasks require co-operative effort: canning and food preservation, foraging for foodstuffs, (mushrooms and blackberries), construction of all kinds, and hunting.

If everyone has a steady job, the team will train on weekends. The schedule ought to include four or five classes taught by specialists. Classes are assigned to team members in their specialties ahead of time. For example:

HANDS ON TRAINING. Rifle practice. Chainsaw uses. Rope usage. Animal control. Mechanical advantages with levers and ropes. Land navigation and terrain analysis.

PROBLEM SOLVING SESSIONS. Have so many trees to cut down, knots to tie and apply, big objects to move with mechanical advantage, or a course at night in the woods. The better these are planned, the more the team learns by doing. Fine details are often what make the most complicated missions successful. Think ahead. Compass courses at night are safer if police whistles are carried, especially for those who zigged when they should have zagged.

Should you train tough? Army Airborne School (at age 35) brought me a lot of pain. Karate was the same; I broke a few bones. (Mostly mine) But through all of that, I became more confident. I recommend that you train as tough as you can, because it breeds confidence, and confidence is the most important survival attitude. If you train really hard, you will know you can make it anywhere in the toughest of circumstances.

But don't, DO NOT, do anything dangerous. If a team member suffers an injury because safety was ignored ("Hey! We train tough; we use live ammunition in OUR exercises.") then the morale of the whole team suffers. Also, the rest of the team has to pick up the additional work load of the missing member, and that member's special skills will probably be most needed during his absence.

Our own training sessions often end with some party time. Usually we have enough refreshments and food to last a couple of hours so that team members interchange in a friendly, relaxed atmosphere. All work and no play tends to give us the grouchies. We not only deserve to have a good time, but the team's morale improves.

Another vast advantage from the social hour comes from the interchange between team members on a one-to-one basis. Very often, some of the stories I have heard during a party get together have taught me some life-saving lessons.

If times ever do get tough, you will appreciate knowing that the teamwork and training you have learned from these four volumes will make the going tremendously easier. If you have practiced what we teach in these four books, and you are working together as a team, severe circumstances won't mean much more to you than a camp out.

FROM EVERYBODY'S KNIFE BIBLE.
Aim your knife at the sun to tell what time it is, or to tell the height of any object, or find the width of a river. We teach you how to drill it and engrave it---and you become a super woods pro.

Section III

INDIVIDUAL OUTDOOR SKILLS

Your team is the sum of its components. If
each member is strong and a skilled outdoorsman,
the team will be super-strong and able to make it
anywhere. In order to make a strong team, each
individual needs to develop certain skills and
outdoor abilities.

In this book, we only talk about the most
basic skills. The other three volumes do much
better; they are designed to bring each individual
to the pinnacle of outdoor excellence.

To be well rounded in the outdoor skills you
need, you should read all three of the books listed
below. You can order by mail from, Pathfinder
Publications, 150 Hamakua, Kailua, HI 96734. If
you let them know you already own one volume, they
will provide free postage and handling.

THE GREEN BERET'S COMPASS COURSE teaches you
to bee-line back to any starting point in the woods
without without getting lost, and you will never
need to use a map again. $6.95

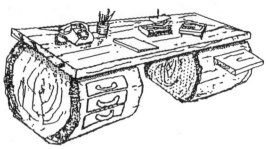

THE GREEN BERETS' GUIDE TO OUTDOOR SURVIVAL, BOOK II is all-around training manual for the individual. Sub-titled, "Great Livin' in Grubby Times," it includes choice of gear, choice of survival weapons, combat gunnery, and escape and evasion. In addition, the book teaches you how to start from scratch in the woods and build super shelter and furniture with your chainsaw. Finally, the book tells you how to build and use handmade weapons in the woods. $12.95

EVERYBODY'S KNIFE BIBLE brings you and your knife up to the 21st century. We figured out a way to aim your hunting knife at the sun and tell what time it is. The rest of the book is much better. You can zip through the woods as if you owned them, scale cliffs, drop trees, and cross rivers successfully because of the all-new information this book puts out. $9.95.

"After his Army discharge, Paul became a successful real estate broker and developer. He made over a half million dollars from 1970 to 77. So, we asked him to write on budgeting."

-Rick Woodcroft-

Chapter 8

SURVIVAL BUDGETING

Nobody should ever write on any subject without reading what everyone else has to say. Even though a writer might know more than anyone else, he just must--make sure.

Besides, we don't think anybody should be in any business without being aware of the competition. Our business is selling information, (which we try to do with comical and sardonic flair so that it entertains). We try to make good on the motto: "None better, few as good." So---we check out the competition.

Some guys just don't get the job done. The editor of a recently published survival manual said, "...this is NOT the last word on survival." Then, in that same manual, a firearms writer wrote, (paraphrased)"...buy a pistol, two rifles and a shotgun, and 17,000 rounds..." I would certainly hope that's not the last word...

Seventeen thousand rounds! I wondered why
they just didn't say, "Buy a tank; what the heck.
They shoot farther--get a deer every time."

We were amazed at how absurd some writers
on survival become. As we thought about it, we
discovered why. The best way to learn anything is
from experience, and apparently, many of the
writers haven't needed to survive yet. Lots of
information in their books and articles is missing.
One such subject is BUDGETING.

Survival budgeting means more than matching
your available money to expenses. It means you
match up, or consider:
1. Supplies and equipment vs money, not only
available cash, but future earnings.
2. Your life span--how long you reasonably plan
to be around to use up your supplies and equipment.
3. Your work span, that is, how much will you earn
before you quit working?
4. Your dependents. How many people will depend
on you? What are your goals for them? For
yourself?
5. What about future needs? Immediate needs?
Does your life style require special habitat
requirements?
6. Will there be any changes in family size?
7. Think about future availability with regard to
items you will need for survival. Should you buy
now or wait til something better comes along?
Will technological advance probably produce a
better one after you spent your money on this first
issue?
8. If you do buy now, think about weight and
logistics. Some of the things I bought a long time
ago have cost me two times as much because they had
to be moved, and/or stored.
9. Training time required?

10. Cost effectiveness. Will the item save you as much in a year as the purchase price?
11. Finally, think maintenance. If you buy something that takes tons of time to repair, then it owns you; you don't own it.

After considering ALL these factors, ask yourself, "What's most important?" Consider need, both current and future. Price and opportunity often make a big difference. Personal likes and dislikes will play a part, of course, even though they frequently mislead.

GREAT FUN, AND PRACTICAL IF YOU LIVE NEAR WATER. BUT A POOR PRE-SURVIVAL BUDGET PURCHASE. REASON: TOO BULKY.

I buy things I might not need if the price is right. For example, I own four double-bitted axes. New, they are worth $18 each. I bought the heads for $3, and the handles for $5. I put the parts together while I watched TV or talked to friends. I use the extra ones for trading stock.

Consider both equipment and supplies. Supplies refers to things that are expendable--to be used up. Equipment refers to things that are used over and over again, such as tools. You will need some supplies before you need equipment. For example: food, water and medicine will always be a pressing necessity. Once you have these items stored, consider books, firearms, and garden implements.

To begin with, change your concept about money, cash, gold or silver. It's an exchange medium, that's all. If our system collapes, it won't matter much when your wife tells you, "I am not overdrawn; you're under-deposited." Dollars may be worthless. In that event, different exchange mediums will operate more effectively.

Winchester Shotgun. Exchangeable? In a survival situation, like gold!

Now, we budget. Subtract your expenses from your income, multiply that figure by the number of earning years remaining in your work life, and set that amount aside for the supplies and equipment you need.

Example: My income: $30,000
            I spend $25,000
            My surplus = $5,000

I'll earn for another 15 years. Therefore: ($5,000 X 15 years = $75,000)

Think also about asset conversion. Sell a toy, or maybe some real estate to generate extra purchasing power. Even if the asset is increasing in value, you may be FAR better off to sell now. Remember the Rockefeller maxim for timing sales:

"You're better off to get out six months too early, than ten minutes too late." Also, your objective is to SURVIVE, not acquire paper wealth that might be of no value.

If you want more money, or purchasing power, increase income, or cut expenses. Perhaps what you save will increase in value after a crash.

You can get a second job, go into business for yourself, or invest. Perhaps your wife and children will work in order to increase income. The great economics writer, John L Springer, once wrote, "If you want to be a successful saver, learn to save money for a purpose.

Exchange mediums are as vast as the products we produce. Pick a few exchange mediums that you know will be in future demand, and store them. Ammunition, silver/gold, and good tools are just some examples. Don't, however, violate logistics laws and hoard a heavy item. You may need to stay mobile.

Another problem is this: most books never mention the labor of reselling or exchanging the products you save. Often, the time it takes to sell or find a good exchange could have been used to earn enough to buy the item new out of a high priced store.

MY
COMPUTER
provides
communication
library access
accounting
data memory
word writing.

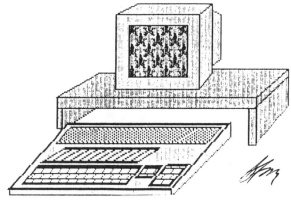

If you want to own the best exchange medium possible, think about acquiring a new, marketable skill. No matter where you go, it goes with you, and you can then trade your skill/hours for food, water, medicine, etc. One survivalist sailor learned how to weld; now, anywhere he goes, he is in BIG demand repairing boats.
86

In my own case, I use computers to produce the books and tapes that Pathfinder sells. In addition, the computer does all kinds of other communication tricks, including flyers, reports, and spread sheets for accounting. I also can manage data, or sell information. With my modem, I can search a thousand magazine articles in under a half hour, no matter where I travel. Even though I buy one today and find that it's worth half as much in a couple of years, the skills I have developed give me a readily available money earner in a crunch.

Finally, observe financial safety margins. Never go into debt so deeply that financial failure could affect nenrves, and thus health. Always leave a margin of safety for the unexpected. Savings are important; you need to deny yourself diligently to provide for an uncertain future.

I've experienced success by trying to apply the christian stewardship approach, which says, in effect: everything---money, time, goods, and health, belong to God and should be used for good. I've been blessed, but more important, I don't sweat it anymore. Let go and let God. It's a great relief to let Somebody Else worry about it all.

How many are in your family? Will your family grow? How long will they live after you? What will they need? What do you want to achieve for them? After sufficient thought, the answers to these questions can be related to income, and at least a monetary budget can be established.

Think, of course, about special equipment you may need for your chosen habitat area. When we moved north, we brought warm clothing. For the South Pacific, I bring dive fins and a pole spear. Short range firearms are inadequate for long range terrain, such as desert. For dense jungle or rain forest, short range firearms are OK; you never see a long range target anyway.

Don't buy things that will be easy to obtain later. You can always obtain cords of firewood when you don't have a steady job. Instead, I stock up on high technology parts which may not be available.

Think about technological advance. I have purchased a few items I thought I couldn't live without, only to find later that the price went down as supplies increased, and the new models were far superior. I wear an old $90 dive watch I can now buy for $24. Guns seem to be an exception. The new models are more cheaply built and don't perform as well as some of the old standards. Many old guns increase in value.

Think about weight. Even if you travel by Mac truck, you can only carry so much gear. Don't be like the Spanish in old Mexico, who loaded their ships so heavy with gold that they sank. Bulk is also a big deal. You have to be able to transport everything you buy. If you don't own a truck, don't buy a diesel generator. More than that, the truck you do own must carry what you buy over some rough terrain, and you can't count on roads.

Never buy anything that will cost hours of time you simply don't have. I've bought things really cheap that required ten hours of repair or construction, and then never found the time.

Consider that you will have more time than usual in the survival mode, and ask yourself if the survival equipment you are buying will be cost effective. I didn't purchase an automatic shotshell reloader because the projected number of needed shells wouldn't warrant the cost of automatic production. However, I spent $3,000 for nail guns once to build an apartment building; they were cost effective on the first job.

Finally, DON'T buy anything you won't be able to MAINTAIN. Sears Roebuck and other large companies now sell appliances with a maintenance contract. I always wondered, "Why I should buy it if they expect it to break?" If you don't have the time, tools, or know-how to repair, either rent or borrow the item from someone else.

As you can see, budget is a big word. It means, "how to think about the collective aspects of your unique situation, and match not only your abilities, but your avail-abilities to your needs. Learn to do this, and you will avoid the 17,000 round syndrome.

I couldn't believe it. Seventeen thousand rounds--and not one mention of a spare firing pin!

Rick spent a lot of time in a lot of places where water was scarce. When you need water, it doesn't matter whether you are in jungle, desert, mountains or forest--you can't call a utility company; you have to figure it out for yourself.

These are some of the tricks he used to keep his team alive in Vietnam.

Chapter 9

MAKING YOUR WATER DRINKABLE
by
Rick Woodcroft

No matter where you go or what you do, you MUST drink water. Water usage could approximate two gallons per man per day, for drinking purposes alone. How much water your team uses will be related to temperature, humidity and the amounts of physical labor they do.

Water is essential for life. Without enough, working in a hot and humid environment increases the risk of becoming a heat casualty. Heat cramps and heat exhaustion are not fun. Moreover, heat stroke is a true medical emergency.

It's important to have more water on hand than you think you will need. That's why government disaster people tell you to fill your bathtubs in an emergency.

The prime factors in choosing the type of water purification you'll need are the number of people in the group and cost. So, we divide this into two main parts, large group solutions and small group, or individual short term solutions.

Your water supply has to be:
PURE & SECURE

No matter what the situation, consider all surface water contaminated. Water may look and smell fine, but be grossly contaminated. On the other hand, it may look and smell terrible and still be drinkable. You just can't tell without a full laboratory analysis. The rule is: When you don't know, TREAT IT.

Water purification and supply requires a variety of talent to produce. It's a shared responsibility of the medic and the engineer. The medic helps in source selection and constantly monitors purity. The engineer helps in site selection too, because it's his job to get water from the source to the delivery point. In addition to the construction of the purification system itself, he may need pipes and pumps.

Water security means you transport your main drinking fluid to your usage point without letting it pick up dirt or germs, and make sure that an enemy can't follow your pipe right into your camp. Worse yet, water supplies can be poisoned.

The Engineer's first task is a feasibility study. Does the group have the time, manpower, material and money necessary to complete the project or must an alternative be found? If the results are positive, then planning, building and maintaining the system becomes one of his most important functions. It takes top priority.

Other engineering considerations are; Protect against surface contamination. Cap or cover wells/springs. Place livestock holding pens, septic systems and solid waste facilities down hill and away from wells. Select a water source with the least amount of turbidity, which doesn't necessarily mean the water is bad; it merely tells you how often you will have to back flush, and change or replace your filter.

The medic tests and monitors the purity of the water. If you have the laboratory facilities, you should monitor for the presence of E. coli. Although the organism isn't harmful in it's own right, it is an indication of fecal contamination.

For individuals and small groups, disinfectants have the advantage of being portable and inexpensive. Water purification tablets are the most common example. They can be purchased on the open market and have directions for use right on the label. READ THE LABEL AND FOLLOW THE DIRECTIONS CAREFULLY. Although disinfectants kill harmful organisms, they have no effect on chemical or nuclear contamination.

Commercially produced "survival" filtration systems not only remove bacterial contaminants, but they remove particulate matter, some chemicals and some nuclear contaminates. Then too, they improve taste. Of course, they are bulkier and more expensive than chemicals. Since they come in disposable cartridges they are only a short term solution.

Some field expedients are also available. Bottled commercial bleach will work. One canteen cap of bleach to one quart of water makes a quart of disinfectant solution. Note well! It does **NOT MAKE** drinking water. Add one capfull of that solution to one quart of water for drinking. Wait 20 minutes if the water is warm or 30 minutes if the water is cold. Boiling is not recommended-- not because it doesn't work, but because practically nobody waits 20 minutes for their water to boil, then cool, before drinking, especially when thirsty.

The best solution for a permanent cooking and drinking water supply is a deep water well or spring. The initial cost can be severe, but in general you have no purification problems. Mother nature has already filtered it for you.

Even though your well or spring is producing a steady supply of water, interruptions can and do occur. Build a storage tank large enough to hold a week's supply of drinking and cooking water. If your pump breaks, don't shower or wash cars. Water rationing for a week may be uncomfortable, but weigh this against the cost of a larger tank. Also, have spare parts or a spare pump available.

All surface waters, moving or still, either have the potential of becoming contaminated, or they actually are. Purifying water can be costly; in addition to the costs of construction, someone will have to learn professional water plant engineering. Because of that, it is normally cheaper to drill a series of wells than it is to set up a water treatment facility.

Training and preparing your team in this area is relatively easy. To be competent survivalists and support their team, the engineer and medic must take the time and effort to tour a water treatment plant. They should ask questions and take notes as to the concentrations of chemicals used. The rest is simple mechanics. The only complicated part is chlorination and floculation.

Water treatment is basically easy to understand. It relies on gravitational flow through filters which progressively remove smaller and smaller particles. Then, the water is chemically treated. Untreated water flows in one end and treated water flows out the other.

Think: Special Forces, First Class, or, SFFC. The letters stand for: SETTLING, FILTRATION, FLOCULATION, AND CHLORINATION. The first step is the reservoir itself. Not only is it a storage place but the really large particles settle out in it. The water is then pumped to a settling tank where baffles slow the flow to the point at which even smaller particles settle out.

Next, the water is allowed to flow through gravel filters which slow the water further and trap even smaller particles. The filtered water then goes to a precipitation tank or floculation chamber where a chemical that forms a sticky compound is added. The compound traps even smaller particles, including some of the bacteria, and then forms a precipitate which sinks to the bottom.

The final step is chlorination. It actually kills the viruses and bacteria. So, as you can see, the process is relatively simple. With this knowledge, plus what you learn on a trip trough an operational plant, you can begin to build your own facility.

Have your engineer screen the intake at the water source to keep out large debris. Pump the water through a "sub sand filter". This consists of:

A layer of coarse rock,
A layer of finer rock,
A layer of coarse gravel,
A layer of fine gravel, and finally,
A layer of sand.

Build it so that it can be back-flushed. How many layers you use, the grit of the gravel and sand, as well as the thickness of the layers depend upon the quality of water at the intake. Since the quality varies so much, your final choices will have to be determined experimentally. Don't bother filtering clean looking water through real coarse rock.

As the filter begins to plug up, the out-flow will gradually decrease. When this happens, back flush with filtered water until the rinse water runs clean. Periodically, it will be necessary to replace the sand and rock layers since back flushing tends to mix the layers together.

Filters can be made out of any non- toxic material that will hold water. In the illustration you can see examples of a 55 gallon drum and a concrete tank. It is obvious that back flushing will eventually ruin the integrity of the layers. A simple way around this is to have separate containers for each grade of filter material.

You may run into some problems at the outlet end of your system. A common error is to use too fine a grade of sand, which compacts, causing a slow-down in the water flow. Another problem occurs when your sand escapes through the outlet.

Correct this by placing the outlet pipe inside another pipe or a can with perforations. Again, a coarser grade of sand may help.

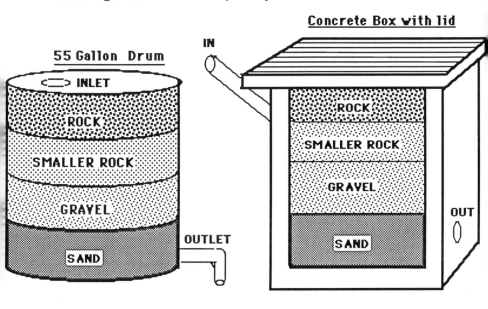

55 Gallon Drum

INLET

ROCK

SMALLER ROCK

GRAVEL

SAND

OUTLET

Concrete Box with lid

IN

ROCK

SMALLER ROCK

GRAVEL

SAND

OUT

    I would use a good commercial swimming pool filter of the diatomaceous earth variety rather than build a flocculation tank. They are sturdy, and have a built in back flush. This system will allow only very small particulates to pass. Make the chlorination tank and the ready for use storage tank drainable from the bottom. Install your supply outlet a foot or so above the tank's bottom.

    Look for ways to decrease the amount of water you need to purify. For instance, water for toilets and radiators can be impure. Consider untreated sources of water for flushing toilets and washing vehicles and clothes. If you cut down on treated water you use, you'll cut down on cost. On the other hand, water for washing dishes and bathing has to be as pure as your drinking water.

The medic is responsible for inspections. He maintains a concentration of 10 parts per million (ppm) of chlorine at the treatment point. If you are getting less than 5 ppm at the tap, you may have a break in the delivery system. If not, you may have a lot of particulates or bacteria at the treatment point. In this case, increase the chlorine (Calcium Hypochlorate) concentration until a level of 5-10 ppm is obtained at the point where water is taken for use (the tap).

The other method of purifying water is distillation. This method removes all contaminants. However, the big problem with distillation is that it takes a lot of energy to turn liquid water into vapor and then recondense it, so distillation is expensive--too expensive to run. Although you can obtain free energy from the sun, the solar stills available today don't turn out enough water for a large group.

Nevertheless, I strongly recommend that everyone learn how to make a solar still because in some of the driest parts of the world solar stills are the ONLY way to get water.

If you can't get water, you can't exist. Once you do find a supply, however, make sure it stays pure. If you do that, you will keep the whole team healthy.

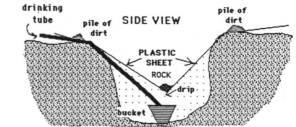

Standard solar pit-still for sucking water out of mother earth. The wider and deeper, the better. The heat under the plastic creates rising mist which condenses on the cool plastic sheet and drips down into the bucket. You drink through the tube.

Rick studied a lot of Judo. In Special Forces, he studied hand-to-hand combat extensively.

"I'll never forget brawling with him for fun on a lawn one day in front of a bunch of Army spectators. I thought I could hip roll him from my right... But he reached between my legs from behind with his left hand and created new, unspeakable pain by squeezing. Then, with his right hand, he grabbed the neck of my jungle fatigues, and turned me up side down. Not too gently, he bounced me on my head. 'You should be careful with that move,' he said.

If I had to study hand to hand combat under anybody, it would be this guy. He is a decorated war hero because he developed an attitude. Knowing is one thing; thinking invincibly is something else. Rick thinks invincibly... Read this, and you will begin to think the same way..."

-Don Paul-

Chapter 10
HAND TO HAND COMBAT
AND SELF DEFENSE
by Rick Woodcroft

Hand to hand combat is nothing more than guerrilla warfare on a smaller scale. The principles are similar. You prepare. You learn what to do, practice and train, and when an emergency arises, you'll survive.

I have been in all kinds of martial arts classes for years. Martial arts instructors teach their particular discipline because that's what they get paid for: their particular skill. I have no argument with that; they paid the price by spending the same long years learning the art themselves. For you, however, that kind of time and effort may not be required.

Look at it this way: Educational systems are organized so that you get a general education before specializing. You graduate from high school before college. Yet, martial artists often teach specific and highly technical methods before teaching general combat principles.

We want to change all that. We want to make you _effective_ by taking the best from several arts.

Take advantage of your personal strengths and compensate for your weaknesses. If you do, you will raise your combat ability far above the average street fighter's, and security will be yours. You just don't need to practice Aikido, Judo, or Karate for years to survive. A few simple moves and some common sense applied will do the job. Of course, you can spend more time and improve.

These are the principles of combat:
I	RANGE
II	STRENGTHS TO WEAKNESSES
III	SUPERIOR POSITION
IV	FIRST STRIKE
V	USE A WEAPON

I.   In hand-to-hand combat the most important principle is RANGE. If you can reach your enemy but he can't reach you, you win. Remember when the Argentinians scored on a British destroyer in the

Falklands with an Exocet missile from a range of forty miles out? The plane wasn't scratched; the ship is sunken history. So it goes--big bore rifles out-range pistols, and Karate kickers' legs can blast a boxer. The guy who can attack from a long range wins.

I RANGE is the distance between combatants. More exactly, it's the distance from your striking surface to your selected target. Let's call the ranges 1,2 and 3. Three refers to the distance at which combatants can kick. (I can't punch you while you are kicking me.) A punch is delivered from a number two range. (I can't grab you while you're punching me.) At a number one range, we are close to each other. Here, grabs, elbow strikes, knee strikes, and palms of the hand are more effective. If somehow you could stay out of range and effectively neutralize me, I lose.

II. Apply your STRENGTHS TO WEAKNESS. We are going to teach you the human body's weak spots. Against those, learn to use your own natural strengths. If you have strong arms, use them. If you're a slender person with a small waist, you will have a great body coiling effect on a reverse punch, so practice that.

III. The principle of SUPERIOR POSITION is also noteworthy. Getting above your opponent has been good strategy since conflict came into existence. Stairs are great for hand-to-hand combat, because it will no longer be hand-to-hand; it's now your foot to his head. Also, guard your back; don't let assailants get behind you. Frequently, fighters lose good combat position by trying too hard and over-extending with some special kick or punch. Surprise...the counter-attack brings pain that only a drugged Hindu could endure.

Good balance is also an important part of superior position. Getting caught off balance or out of position renders you useless. Without balance, you are without power---neither in blocking nor attack. But if you have full balance in a fighting stance, you can easily defend yourself.

IV.   Finally, the FIRST STRIKE principle means a lot.   Get their "fustus with the mostest" (General Jubal Early, Confederate Army) is good advice. Even if you take some blows, they won't be delivered effectively from a damaged opponent. Don't wait for a situation to develop; either retreat or attack, but in either case, BE FIRST!

V.   Some WEAPONS are better because they increase range, such as a tonfa or a bo. Others bring the focused force of a blow down to a smaller striking point, and therefore inflict greater pain and injury, such as a knife or Yawara stick. Still, other weapons increase your force and leverage, such as a baseball bat. Above all, ANY WEAPON IS BETTER THAN NO WEAPON.

Basically, a WEAPON is:

ANYTHING THAT:
LENGTHENS OR STRENGTHENS
YOUR SPHERE OF DEFENSE

In Volume II of this series, the chapter on Handmade Weapons said it another way and added some extra maxims for combat training. Emergency weapons are lying around you all of the time. You merely have to think about it. A rock or stick is obvious, but how about taking off your sock and filling it with sand and rocks?

In an urban environment, you are surrounded by glass, which, when freshly broken, has an edge that puts a razor to shame. You can clamp the glass carefully in your hand, or use your shirt as a knife handle. It won't stab well, but it will slice cleanly. If you "borrow" some glass from a commercial building with a burglar alarm, help will probably arrive soon.

Engagement of an enemy in hand to hand combat is only done as a last resort. The whole purpose of a survivalist is to continue to be a survivor. Avoidance is the byword. Do not be afraid to run or hide. MACHO doesn't survive; ALIVE does.

Rules. There is only one rule: win at all cost. Almost always, flight before fight is better. If you can't escape, negotiate. Finally, if you can't negotiate, go to war--and WIN. If a fight is inevitable, do it the same way you would execute a raid. Take advantage of surprise, and attack violently. Then, disengage and get away.

Now, add three new concepts:
Target selection,
Striking surface selection, and
Method of delivery.

Target selection is primarily influenced by the degree of damage you wish to inflict. Regardless of circumstance, you must know what you are hitting and why, so study human anatomy. Other factors in target selection are:

Your opponent's body position. Everyone fights differently. Nobody covers everything. See what's available. It's like reading a menu in a restaurant; various targets are there, but you may have to pay a heavy price to chew one up.

101

A weapon, or lack of one. Some weapons
require two hands and so cannot be wielded without
exposing prime target areas. Other weapons,
however, (in the hands of a trained combatant)
expose very little.

Your own competence. Finally, never go for a
target you're not sure how, or where, to hit.
Several weak spots on the human body are located
next to fortified areas. For example, if you miss
a temple shot and hit a forehead with a fist, you
probably will break YOUR hand.

If you pick one target area of the body, you
can simplify your training. For example, study
only the leg's targets and the striking surfaces of
the foot. Practice and study. Keep it simple.

On your second training day, review and
practice the first day's lesson. Pick a new
striking surface such as the elbow. Practice blows
to chest and abdomen. After you can hit all of the
targets with a few simple techniques, then, and
only then, add new procedures.

Avoid techniques which are likely to cause
injury. Don't use hard blocks; deflect. Severely
bruised forearms can cause you to become gun shy.
Also you absolutely have to use a harder striking
surface than the selected target. For example, use
fingers against the eyes only. A broken finger may
be nothing to you right now, but in a survival
situation it could set up a chain reaction leading
to your death.

Don't learn to kick higher than your own
chest. If a movie star misses a high kick, they
re-shoot the scene. If you miss a high kick, your
opponent will re-shoot your groin.

As you begin training, refer to the charts and diagrams.

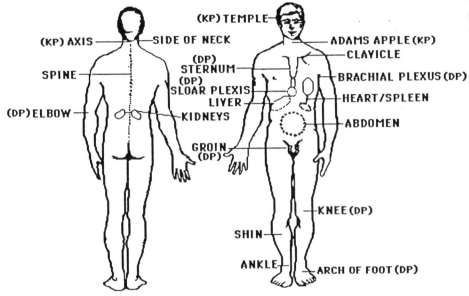

(KP) TEMPLE
(KP) AXIS — SIDE OF NECK
SPINE
(DP) ELBOW
(DP) STERNUM
(DP) SLOAR PLEXIS
LIVER
KIDNEYS
GROIN (DP)
ADAMS APPLE (KP)
CLAVICLE
BRACHIAL PLEXUS (DP)
HEART/SPLEEN
ABDOMEN
KNEE (DP)
SHIN
ANKLE
ARCH OF FOOT (DP)

* (PP) ALL OTHER LABELED POINTS

We use three designations for target selection:
PP for Pain Producer
DP for Disabling Point
KP for Killing Point

With regard to killing points, it's best to know what exactly causes death, because most hand-to-hand deaths are caused accidentally. We feel that if you know the tragedy of the damage you can cause, you will be less likely to kill, and more likely to use disabling and pain producing techniques.

Head--Nasal bones.

You hear a lot about driving the nasal bones into the brain. People who don't know anatomy dreamed this up. The nasal bones are small and delicate--much more so than the basilar bone of the skull, so the nasals will splinter and collapse when hit hard. The collapse causes severe pain and tearing, but it won't kill. So, palm-of-the-hand to nose is only a very good DISABLING blow.

Head-- Temporal-Parietal Sulcus

The temporal and parietal bones join each other on each side of the head. Where they come together, they form a special kind of joint called a suture. Immediately inside the skull and directly below this joint runs the Middle Meningeal artery. The bones of the skull here are very thin and are further weakened by the suture. This point is located one inch above and one inch forward of the ear. A strong blow at this point causes the bones to shatter, severing the artery. Bleeding causes an increase in pressure inside the skull which puts pressure on the brain. Brain damage is almost inevitable; death may result.

I would be remiss in my responsibilities if I didn't give a strong warning about blows to the head. Any blow to the head may cause death or brain damage.

Under the impetus of fear or anger, your body releases adrenalin. Adrenalin gives you a lot of extra strength. Fighting with adrenalin coursing through your veins will increase the chance of inducing serious injury EVEN THOUGH it was not your intention.

The second thing to consider is that you do
not have to deliver a blow strong enough to break
the skull to cause death or serious injury. The
brain actually floats within the cranial cavity.
Because of inertia, the brain tends to stay in
place when the head is struck. The skull, however,
is moving, and thus strikes the brains. Severe
injury may result.

Neck--Craico-Thyroid Cartilage
This is commonly known as the voice box, or
Adams apple. Even a moderately forceful blow to
this structure will crush it. Death ensues when
the blood in the lungs and/or the ruined airway
causes suffocation.

Neck-- Strangulation
A well executed choke hold not only cuts off
the air supply (slow strangulation), it cuts off
the blood supply to the brain by blocking the blood
flow throughout the Jugular Veins and the Carotid
Arteries. It is quick and painless. Death
results from a lack of oxygen to the brain.

Neck-- The Atlas and Axis
These are the first two cervical vertebrae.
Death and instant paralysis occur when two bones
make contact with and damage the Medulla Oblongata
(Brain Stem), so a blow to the back of the neck is
dangerous.

The Thorax--
All blunt object trauma to any part of the
Thorax can be fatal depending on the force of the
blow. Bone splinters cause bleeding and lung
collapse. The most vulnerable target areas are the
sternum, collar bone and lower edge of the rib
cage. For example, when you shatter a collar bone
(the clavicle), it becomes splintered. The jagged
ends of the splintered bone puncture the sub-

clavian artery and the lung itself. That produces severe bleeding and a hole in a sack that's designed to hold air. Blood and air between the chest-wall and the lungs will cause lung collapse.

STRIKING SURFACES

Striking surfaces are chosen by comparing the hardness of the striking surface with the hardness of the target. If you select a target that is harder than your striking surface, you lose. Don't try breaking someone's sternum with your fingers, for example, you'll only crunch your little digits.

The forehead and back of the skull are hard, so they can smash into someone else's face. This is a good defense against a bearhug. In this situation, use a knee or heel to the groin in combination with head butts.

Don't forget your teeth. You can bite anything, but particularly good targets are the nose, ears and upper lip. (Remember--there is no such thing as fair.)

The elbow is an extremely hard striking surface that can be used against all targets above the waist. Avoid hitting the forehead and back of the skull with your elbow, however, unless you want to splinter your arm.

The hand is the most versatile weapon at the disposal of the unarmed fighter. The number of ways to use it would require a complete book. Here, only the simplest, safest and easiest striking surfaces are listed.

The fist is the most widely known striking surface. It's effective, but you have to make one correctly. With your fingers extended straight out from your palm, close the first two finger joints only. Then roll the closed fingers into the palm of the hand and place your thumb safely out of the way under the first two fingers. Press up and in hard against your fingers with your thumb. Make sure the fist is closed very tightly. By doing so you are using muscle and adjacent bones as a splint, thus reducing the possibility of fracturing your hand. Keep the wrist flat and locked on an imaginary line running from the elbow to the second knuckle.

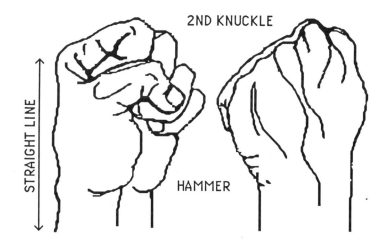

The properly formed fist presents two excellent striking surfaces. The first and second knuckle can be used against any target except very heavy bones such as the forehead. Hammer fists employ the fist's bottom surface. You can hit just about anything with this surface without fear of injury, but the broader surface spreads the force of impact, thus reducing the power delivered on point.

The use of the open hand is limited to specialized targets since it is not as strong as the closed hand (fist). Make the hand rigid by locking the wrist. (See illustration 5.) and by trying to make the little finger and thumb touch as the fingers are slightly cupped.

Use the palms of the hand to hit the ears, simultaneously. If you do this correctly, you will cause the ear drums to rupture.

The knife edge hand can be used against the adams apple, clavicle, side of the neck and the atlas/axis. Note, however, that ALL of these <u>are killing points.</u>

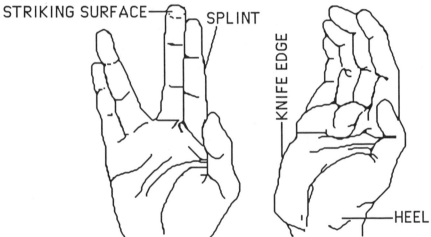

STRIKING SURFACE · SPLINT · KNIFE EDGE · HEEL

As we mentioned earlier, the eyes are the only recommended target for fingers. To strike the eyes, spread the fingers as shown in illustration 6. The index and small fingers support and re-inforce the actual striking fingertips. Practice popping either hand into this position. The strike doesn't have to penetrate far, but should be aimed at an area behind the forehead, and land just under the eyes to "slide" in. That guarantees a score, and the fight's over...

To strike with the heel of the palm; form an open hand and bend your wrist slightly backwards. Recommended targets are the point of the chin and the nose. If you miss the chin, you probably will hit the nose.

The knee is an incredibly strong striking surface and the quadriceps muscle is one of the largest and strongest muscles in the body. To land a knee solidly is to devastate your opponent. Targets are limited only by your ability to reach them. For a knee shot, you've got to get in close.

Like the knee, the foot is a quadriceps-powered delivery system; it's very powerful. The foot has two great advantages over the knee. It has four striking surfaces and is thrown from greater range. The foot then provides a variety of delivery selections and increases your safety margin. One maxim of target selection is this: "If you can reach it, kick it." As I've said before, DO NOT kick over the height of your own chest because over extension can cause loss of balance and VITAL exposure.

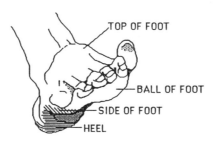

109

To review---first, hand to hand combat is like warfare, the only rule is win. Avoid it if you can but if you must fight, do it violently and quickly.

Think: I   RANGE
        II   STRENGTHS TO WEAKNESSES
        III   SUPERIOR POSITION
        IV   FIRST STRIKE
        V   USE A WEAPON

Engage your enemy at the maximum range possible. Exploit all of your opponent's weaknesses. Use the most effective technique available to you. Get into position, and go for it. When this fight is over, you will still be around, so age before beauty; take the first shot---and, HIT HARD. Any weapon is better than no weapon.

Learning about striking surfaces and targets is education. Books educate; instructors train. You need both. You must practice what you have learned. To be really effective, you must have someone show you how to kick, punch and choke.

Still, knowing the principles of hand-to-hand combat and the basic striking techniques will provide you with a good margin of emergency safety. Think flight before fight, but if you have to fight, stay uninjured and survive.

"For three years, we lived on an Oregon farm. We had several dogs during those years, and we also tried raising every other kind of critter. At one time we had over five hundred rabbits. We learned things every survivor should know."

I interviewed Thies and Ann Mesdag, owners of Von Nassau Kennels in Washington. They developed a German Shepherd with a nose that only poor cocaine could appreciate. They sold the breed to the Air Force, and successive offspring were Vietnam heroes.

--Don Paul

Chapter 11

Using God's gift to man...ANIMALS
to double your survive-ability.

Scripture says God gave us, "...dominion over all the beasts of the earth." Animals were put here to help, and God made them so they could do some tremendous tricks---far beyond man's capability.

As you may know, for example, the U.S. Navy has been hanging pigeons in a cage beneath a helicopter because they can see many times farther than man. Pigeons have saved a lot of lives.

Of course, dogs patrol, defend, herd, attack, carry, pull, rescue, lead the blind and a do variety of other useful tricks. Dogs are amazing. Certain breeds are smarter than others, but they all respond to training.

It's never been tried before, but big birds could probably be trained to carry cameras and do air photo reconnaissance and small bomb delivery. (I've been bombed by pigeons in Paris before.)

What's the bottom line? Animals can partner up with you to give you super-human ability. Horses are stronger, dogs are faster, pigeons fly home, and hawks have eyes you wouldn't believe. Learn to train your animal, and its best God-given ability is yours for the price of care and feed. Learn to raise other animals, and you can eat like a king.

If survival for you means no gas, then it means no motored vehicles, and you will need a partner stronger than yourself. Learn about horses; I have found it rather easy. Besides hauling your body through rough terrain, they can lift loads of anything laterally or in the air, (using a pulley wheel).

I rode my horse everywhere. We spent so much time together we often smelled alike. A couple of times, I was able to shoot a deer with a bow and arrow. We walked right up on them.

I would sleep in a hammock bundled up in a deep freeze sleeping bag, and my horse (blanketed) would stay right with me. (Oats and apples help). Horses survive by flight, and through the ages have learned the advantage of an early start. (Maybe that's why pastors claim that late church-goers have no horse sense.) Anyway...you want to sleep soundly, so tell your horse to wake you up if danger approaches. Tie his halter to some tin cans, and if his head jerks up to listen, the tin cans will wake you right up. It beats listening to your hound bark and bay at the moon all night. After my horse and I spent some time together, I understand why some people are horse lovers.

Horses cost a lot of money and eat a lot more grass than cows do, so you have to pay for them. They need shoeing from time to time, and they are a touchy animal, often requiring vet work. If a horse is too expensive for you, you should try a dog. Dog spells g-o-d backwards. I think it's because they love and keep on loving, no matter what you do.

We raised a horse and dog together, and took both on long trips. They got along fine. The dog quit nipping at the horse's heels after one kick, and they learned to like each other.

I had a German Shepherd with a Phd degree once. She would chase sheep and goats off my front lawn on my command.

She also scored big in dog bite. Her best bite was on a car burglar in Southern California. He got in the car all the way before she attacked, and the blood trail went clear across the parking lot into the brush. Her worst bite occurred when I sold my house and forgot to show her the closing date on the papers. As the new owner was bent over unpacking, she came in through a window and bit him... well, let's just say she proved the gentleman wasn't as well reared as he thought.

Dogs are either trained to be guard dogs or attack dogs. The former guards property. The latter goes after enemies on command. It's commonly believed that the two mix, but you're better off to stick with one or the other.

Although I prefer big dogs, the small variety does really well for a lot of jobs, such as chasing rabbits. Still, you can train a big dog to do the same. I fed a doberman puppy raw rabbit for awhile, and turned him loose in wild rabbit

113

country.   I had taught him to halt and   stay,   and
got   him   to do it close on the tail of   a   rabbit.
When the rabbit got far enough away, I shot.

Another   dog's   best trick was to   go   home
from   anywhere.   He was a black lab, and   I   could
write   notes   home.   After he delivered,   he   would
find me again.   Amazing.

Dog   owners need two personality qualities.
You must be PATIENT & FIRM.   Make sure the   animal
knows   you say what you mean and mean what you say,
and success will be yours.

If   you   want   an   alarm   animal,   consider
geese.   We   had a few in our front yard   and   they
never   failed to announce a visitor.   They   require
only a little   feed and a little maintenance.

Some animals solve problems for you.   A ton
of mice lived in our barn until we bought a   couple
of   kittens.   In Hawaii,   though,   they had a   rat
problem, so the mongoose was imported. One hunts by
night--the other by day; both flourish, so now they
have a mongoose problem too.

If   you think "partner" you will discover a
lot   more about animal usage than you ever   thought
possible.   Start with a young animal, and it   will
be   helpful   for   a lot of   your   life   span.   Most
animals   die sooner than humans. Sad, I've   know   a
lot of animals with better character than humans.

ANIMALS FOR FOOD
In the finest restaurants, you are   offered
a   list   of various animal carcasses to   eat   from.
Raise   your own; they will taste better.   The   best
leg   of   lamb I ever ate in my life   came   from   a
neighbor's   sheep. I also bought a half   cow   every
year   from   a preacher I knew.   I learned to   like

goat meat in Mexico. Since domestic animals are developed on pure feed without steroids, it not only tastes better, it IS better.

All of the above illustrate a point; you can count on having food around if you raise livestock. What you raise depends on what you like, and also what kind of land you live on. Goats feed on anything. Sheep graze, as do cattle, so you need a little more land. Water is your most difficult problem with just about any livestock you raise. For example, rabbits almost drink their weight daily, and pigs "pig out" on it.

If you don't own a lot of land but you have a good water supply, go with rabbits, especially in a cool climate. I raised Rex and New Zealand Whites for over three years. Not only are they great eating, but they drop the best fertilizer I ever used. If you introduce earthworms into the fertilizer, you get a double benefit. Worm droppings, called castings, are the absolute best for plant growth and the worms aerate the soil. That's not to mention the abundance of fish bait.

I enjoyed rabbits. At one time I had my favorite Rex mama living right outside my office window, and we became good friends. I worked while she took care of her babies. She was a good mother, too.

Rabbits are defenseless, but they breed in big numbers. The whole experience settles around the females, who come into heat often and breed easily. Once bred, it takes 30 days for them to deliver a litter of 8-12, and a good mother raises all her young until they are weaned about four weeks later. In the meantime, you can breed her again. Feed them well if you breed often; I always kept a fresh supply of carrots for new mothers.

You lift a female's tail gently and pull down on the fur around the vulva to check for distention and color. Big and red means she is ready, and you simply move HER (not the buck) into the BUCK'S cage. The mating is fast and the climax is unmistakable.

Note the day on which the mating took place. Then, 27 or so days later, just before the doe is due for delivery, put a nest box in her cage full of sawdust or hay on newspapers. She will pull a lot of hair out of her chest and a few days later, presto! Baby bunny land.

Don't touch the babies unless you wear rubber gloves. Some mothers abandon young who smell like humans. Rabbit mothers also abandon their young if they are disturbed by predators.

If you come up with dead rabbit babies, you know that something is bothering the mothers, and it's time to wire the hutches for sound and keep a loaded .22 handy. We used a cheap $24 intercom that was pretty sensitive. Rabbits thump hard on the floor of their cages when disturbed. That's your signal to get up and eliminate whatever is bothering them.

You can set up an automatic watering system rather easily with plastic pipe. For a dollar or so you can buy a "dew dropper," which is nothing more than a ball check in a tube. The bunny will lick the ball, and water under a few pounds pressure will pour into its mouth. They get ONE cup of feed a day, NO MORE, and they convert this to the best low-fat, white meat imaginable.

Rabbits can also be fed cheaply. You can always scrounge fruit, especially at the end of the picking season. I gathered enough pears and apples to feed my rabbits for six months. Some of the fruit softened and turned into an alcoholic mush, but they loved it! Fresh grass clippings are also free and fun. Rabbits also like hay, and they were especially fond of corn husks, silk, and corn cobs. Toss in an ear of corn, husk and all, and they eat everything but the cob-center, which you can use all summer to clean the bugs off your windshield.

The most feed/growth efficient time to butcher is 3 months after birth. Although a chicken or duck takes me a long time to kill 'n clean, I can get in and out of a rabbit in under seven minutes. Almost all four legged animals clean and gut the same way, so practicing on a rabbit will make you proficient as a field hunter. Here is how someone with over five hundred rabbits on his resume does the job:

Rabbit punch it. If you're weak, use a club and hit just behind the skull to produce a painless demise. Hang the carcass with its stomach toward you, hind legs high. Cut through fur and skin around each leg, then down each leg to join at the middle of the genitals. Now the skin peels easily down over the head. The front paws pop loose as you peel, and the head becomes encased in the body skin. Cut the head off. Next, with a sharp blade turned towards you, slit down the stomach lining and the entrails will fall outward. Cut these from behind. You can cut through the aitch bone at the cartilage junction easily, and spreading the back legs allows you to remove the whole intestine intact. You're left with a headless, skinned carcass with four paws. Smack the furry paws off with a cleaver or hatchet. Elapsed time, about 4 minutes.

Hang head down. Cut around hind legs, then dotted line. Hide peels off warm animals by pulling.

Move to the (harvest) kitchen for 3 minutes more. Cut the diaphram around the edges to expose heart, lungs and liver. Rear quarters severe easily at the pelvic ball-joint and the forequarters do the same. That leaves a back and a thorax (chest). Cut through the thick meat just behind the last rib, bend and break the backbone, then cut through. Done. Final product: four legs, back, thorax, and flanks. Taste: fantastic.

We also raised chickens. Fresh eggs were great, but the chickens began roosting in the rabbit hutches, and the chickens' droppings got into rabbit feed, creating sickness. We got rid of the chickens.

Not only will you enjoy animals a lot once you get to know them, but you will find that they can be great helpers. Just encourage them to do what they naturally can do, and use their talent for your benefit.

Animals provide either services or great meat and other by-products. Either way, in service or in food, animals are worth every invested dime.

Section IV

ALL ABOUT BODY HEAT
FIRE AND SHELTER

Almost all outdoor survival skill books teach a lot of different ways to build a fire. That's not the way to go.

Fire can do some nice things in the woods--- like keeping you from stiffening out due to excessive cold, thus increasing your life span.

But you won't build the correct fire unless you understand WHY you are building it, and most outdoor books never explain that. Fail to understand how fire can work for you, and you may suffer from hypothermia.

This is your major military mission:

GET WARM AND STAY WARM.

Here's how: Learn to understand how your body heat system works.

As I mentioned before, Green Berets spend a lot of time studying. We read A LOT. In all my reading, I have never seen anyone make the human body's heat transfer system easy to understand.

But I think I can do that for you. Learn this one word:

BRACE

It stands for:

BREATHING, RADIATION, AIR CONVECTION, CONDUCTION, and EVAPORATION

The code word is important. To stay warm and healthy, you need to stop heat from leaving your body in all five ways.

If you don't know the theory supporting the reasons for good fire and sufficient shelter, then building both may be futile, followed by fatal.

Face it; freezing to death is un-cool...

A
(Air Convection)

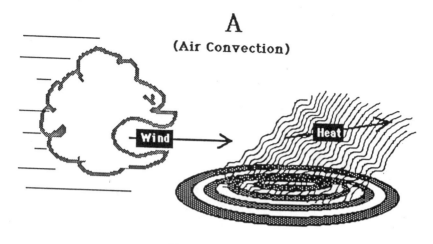

_____

Chapter 12

UNDERSTANDING HEAT TRANSFER
IN OUTDOOR LIFE

If you took the time to learn the code word,
B-R-A-C-E
you are going to find life in the woods much
easier, and safer, too. Now, let's examine what
the letters stand for.

BREATHING
You BREATHE in cold air, and exchange the hear
(from blood) in your tongue, windpipe, and lungs.
Then you exchange that (blood-warmed) air for new,
cold air. This is the major cooling method for
dogs; when they get hot, they pant.

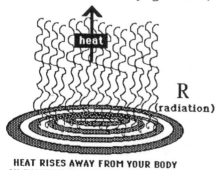

R
(radiation)

HEAT RISES AWAY FROM YOUR BODY
IN EXACTLY THE SAME WAY AS IT DOES
FROM THIS STOVE BURNER. TRAP YOUR
BODY HEAT TO STAY WARM, DON'T LET IT
RADIATE AWAY.

RADIATION
If you bend down
and take a look at a
stove burner or hot car
hood on a summer day,
you will see heat waves
rising. That's
RADIATION. Your body
does the same.

121

• WIND CHILL FACTOR

If the wind blows at this velo-city (MPH):	...and the thermometer reading in degrees F is:								...you are actually exposed to this temperature:
↓	50	40	30	20	10	0	−10	−20	−30
5	48	37	27	16	6	− 6	−15	−26	−36
10	40	28	16	2	− 9	−22	−33	−45	−58
15	36	22	9	− 6	−18	−33	−45	−60	−72
20	32	18	3	− 9	−25	−40	−53	−68	−82
25	30	16	0	−15	−29	−45	−59	−75	−88
30	28	13	− 2	−18	−33	−49	−63	−78	−94
35	27	11	− 4	−20	−35	−52	−67	−83	−98
40	26	10	− 6	−22	−37	−54	−69	−87	−100

AIR CONVECTION

When cold air sweeps by the surface of your skin and steals the heat away, we call it air convection. The instant new heat arrives at the skin's surface, it leaves in a breeze. Result: your temperature drops mighty quick. When the weatherman says it's 17 degrees farenheit and the wind chill factor brings it to -28 degrees Farenheit, he's trying to tell you something...

"Heat loss from air convection may be fatal."

CONDUCTION

This occurs when your warm body touches something cold. That's why sleeping on the bare cold ground numbs your bones.

Your normal body temperature is 98.6 degrees Farenheit. If it contacts anything colder, heat will exchange at that contact point.

Jump into water, (72 degrees warm), and your body heat will leave you in New York minute, (happens quick!) SCUBA manuals say we lose body heat in water 25 times faster than we do in air.

122

EVAPORATION

Finally, when the surface of your skin is even slightly moist, you lose heat by EVAPORATION. Hot perspiration steams off, leaving colder moisture to draw off your body's heat.

******

NOW! This is what you MUST DO. Stop any of the BRACE factors from operating in and around your body and stay warm. In addition, figure out how to use the BRACE factors to ADD heat to, or create heat for, either your body or surrounding atmosphere.

Of course, the seven "P" principle applies. (Prior Proper Planning Prevents Pitifully Poor Performance.) Given a BRACE induced heat reduction in your body, you'll shiver. Good; involuntary muscular exertion warms the body. But it also burns calories.

My bear hunting buddy, Jim Minter, built shelter for his dogs in winter, and his dog food bill dropped dramatically. That warmed his heart---and did the same for the dogs' tails. The hounds didn't need to put in as many calories when their bodies were warmer.

When I was taking SCUBA lessons in Oregon during January, we dove in a 35 degree ocean. Whenever we became cold, we swam around for awhile to heat up our bodies. In the mountains, a brisk walk up a hill will do about the same thing.

However, it's better if you take in warmth from an outside source. This is especially true in a survival situation, because, just as it did for the hound dogs, generating heat burns calories, which you may not have enough food to replace.

123

That's why the legendary Brian Adams loves grub worms; (Book II) they contain fat which adds calories to the diet.

Of course, you can't stop breathing in cold air. But you can drink hot liquids for a looong, relaxing time, and breathe across the top of the cup as you enjoy sipping the drink.

Radiation can be stopped by wearing proper clothing. I never fail to look at an outdoor catalog that doesn't have some fairy model posing in an outdoor jacket. Smashing---quite dashing.

But dressing for style doesn't get it in the woods. You have two functions to consider. Protect your body from weather elements and allow your own perspiration to escape.

The new dress-for-cold theory is the VBI (Vapor Barrier Insulation) theory, but I still like the old layer theory better. Twenty years ago in Germany, I bought an old Army Poncho and had it precisely tailored to fit my torso. Toasty warm. Then, about ten years ago I wore it as I chased a big buck through the snow in Northern California, and got sweaty, then REAL COLD. My sweat started to freeze!

If you succeed in containing your body heat, but you don't get rid of the moisture that follows with exertion, you're gonna have a real problem. The layer theory simply says, "keep piling on more clothes until you feel comfortable; comfort is Nature's way of telling you that radiation heat loss has slowed down.

AIR CONVECTION is little more than radiation at a rapid rate. You generate heat waves (like a hot car hood), and the breeze or wind steals them away so that new body heat slips into the cold vacuum again immediately. Wind chill is now so well defined that weathermen equate wind chill factors to actual temperature. That's because air convection heat loss with a strong wind at 15 above would be the same at a static-wind 20 below. Guaranteed, you'll be losing calories.

Stop this heat theft by adding special (windbreaker) clothing that wind won't penetrate. Once again, though, you have to worry about not letting your body moisture build up inside your clothing so it doesn't escape. Gore-Tex is one popular fabric that does just that. It keeps the rain off your body but lets your own body moisture sift out through the fabric.

If you want to experience CONDUCTION, lay down on cold concrete. You will actually feel the heat departing from your frame. Anything you touch with your bare hands, feet, or head will draw heat out of your body.

ℂ
(Conduction)

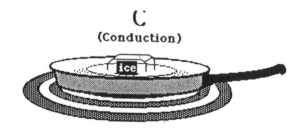

125

The real problem occurs for people who sleep on the ground. If forced into that situation, I use a pair of SPACE blankets (about $9.50 each). They reside permanently in my rucksack. I sandwich them around my sleeping bag with an overlap at the foot-end of the bag.

Too much EVAPORATION can kill you. Dunk your body in a swimming pool on a windy day with a T-shirt on, and then stand in the wind to get the message. If you do get wet, you MUST take your wet clothing off, and get into dry clothing immediately.

ANY WHICH WAY YOU CAN, GET WARM AND STAY WARM. Work at it. Plan ahead. Be diligent. Prevent the B-R-A-C-E factors from stealing your body heat and your life. Too little too late, and you'll stiffen up---then croak.

WHAT HAPPENS WHEN YOU FREEZE

If you're an average human being, you will put things off 'til the last minute. The last minute with frostbite or hypothermia will either maim your body or kill you. Therefore, it's a good idea to predict when the last minute will arrive.

Two disastrous things happen to your body as a result of excessive heat loss. In the first case, only part of your body deep freezes---we call it FROSTBITE. In the second case, you lose the whole bowl of Fritos; the complete body goes into deep freeze; we call that HYPOTHERMIA.

Frostbite occurs due to one or more of the five BRACE factors robbing heat from your body. Blood vessels of the body constrict to send warmth to the vital, inner organs. That problem is often compounded with a little exterior help---such as poor circulation in general, or clothing so tight that circulation is reduced. Either way, the surface areas of the body freeze, especially the extremities: feet, hands, nose, ears and face. Luckily, they also change color to yellow, white, or blue in blotches. If you're smart and travel in pairs, this is the time when a buddy will probably save your life.

Watch Out! With a little stupidity, frostbitten people may try to rectify the problem by overheating the afflicted area. NO-NO, chilly willy! Since the nerves in that area are also frozen, you don't have nature's way of letting you know you are bar-b-queuing your feet. Many people have actually over-cooked their frozen flesh and killed it---dead---forever.

If the frost bites you, you need to secure proper medical treatment inside a **warmed** shelter. Once frostbitten and thawed, the afflicted body part will hurt too severely to be of much use anyway. Also, and get this, WHEN THE FROSTBITTEN AREA THAWS, THE TISSUE SECRETES A FLUID. FREEZE IT ONE MORE TIME, AND YOU CAN KISS THAT RE-FROZEN PORTION OF YOUR CORPUS BYE-BYE. So---you need to stay warm and comfy 'til you heal.

The case #2 scenario is a lot worse... When you lose even more heat and your inner core temperature drops, pray; you are facing death. The inner core of the body is like a delicate computer that requires proper temperature. A few degrees off, and your nervous system fails.

What's the cure? Reverse body heat loss by using the brace factors to pump heat INTO your body. Warm up the core of the body with an outside source of heat. Drink hot liquids. Cling together in a sleeping bag with one or more warm bodies. Dogs are great for this because their bodies are always warmer than ours. But any animal will do, as you will soon find out when you get chilly enough. A couple of times, I've been frigid enough to try hugging a porcupine!

Of course, see a doctor ASAP.

But Benjamin Franklin wrote: "An ounce of prevention is worth a pound of cure." If you learn the BRACE factors, you will know how to **PREVENT** heat theft from your body. In addition, you will know how to compensate for heat loss by adding heat to your body from an outside source. So what it all burns down to is this: You need to learn to build a fire or shelter quickly, anywhere, anytime.

Not only will a fire create warmth, but it will also neutralize parasites and bacteria in a lot of food. Finally, most wild animals are afraid of heat, so your fire pit can be shaped to keep away all kinds of intruders, especially visiting snakes.

So read on... You are going to learn how to build just the fire you need for every occasion.

HOT RIVER ROCKS WITH SMOOTHER EDGES HOLD HEAT UNDER A SANDY BED SURFACE AND KEEP YOU WARM ALL NIGHT LONG.

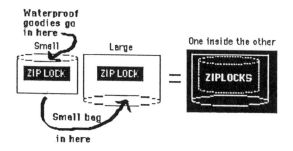

KEEP YOUR FIRE-MAKINS' DRY
WITH TWO ZIPLOCK BAGS.

Waterproof
goodies go
in here

Small   Large   One inside the other

ZIP LOCK   ZIP LOCK   =   ZIPLOCKS

Small bag
in here

Chapter 13

ALL ABOUT FIRE

Almost all Boy Scout and survivor books teach the fire-bow. We don't. We think it's a good idea to learn however, because being able to make a fire with nothing gives you the outdoor confidence you need. No matter how your situation develops, fire, the food, warmth, and safety it provides will always be a psychological comfort.

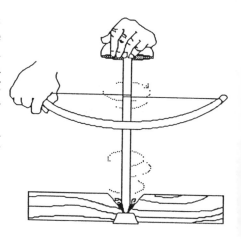

Lots of outdoor books merely teach a dozen or more ways to build a fire. You could go to the trouble of learning the different ways to start a fire from nothing. I don't think it's a good idea. In modern times, "think convenience", especially when convenience doesn't weigh much.

Any or all of these fire starters will work just fine: a cigarette lighter (fuel supply visible), windproof matches, long handle wood matches (for reaching inside a large can), a metal match, (modern version of flint and steel) and some fine steel wool to catch the sparks it creates. A can of sterno is great, and sawdust soaked in diesel oil, then packed into an airtight vitamin bottle, works swell.

Try ALL of these. Learn how to start fires with them. This is one area of expertise that requires a LOT of practice. Then, after you have tried them ALL, pick the three that work best for you, and pack these in your rucksack. I use a waterproof, sealed baggie as double insurance against water intrusion. That way, I am absolutely sure that no matter what kind of capsizing, flooding, or continuous rain I endure, I will ALWAYS be able to start a fire.

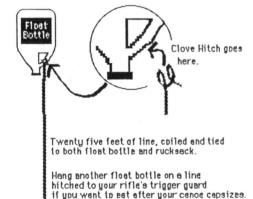

Float Bottle

Clove Hitch goes here.

Twenty five feet of line, coiled and tied to both float bottle and rucksack.

Hang another float bottle on a line hitched to your rifle's trigger guard if you want to eat after your canoe capsizes.

If you canoe, prepare to capsize. Attach your ruck sack to a float bottle and 25 ft of parachute cord. That way, if you do capsize, you can still recover your ruck, and your fire making goodies will still be dry and potent.

Now that you know how to start a fire, you need to learn how to build one.

First, think safety. Granted, I've been so cold I thought about burning down the whole forest. But you really don't want to do that. Be careful. There's no sense in burning down the whole forest just because you were cold. Almost the same as your body loses heat, fires go out of control. They radiate, are subject to wind, conduct, and ignite grass or twigs when conduction is hot enough.

So, prevent your fire from losing heat; contain it. Remove flammable material from around your fire pit; surround it with rocks if you can. Let nothing above the flames ignite, and keep your burnable gear far away. Then, in case you fail, be prepared to add some cold--for example, a bucket of water, or a shovel-full of snow or dirt.

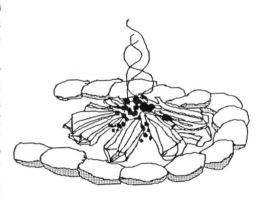

Once safe, don't let your fire fail. Starting a fire successfully presents a problem in progression. A blaze occurs because tinder ignites, kindling catches, and your fuel burns, IN THAT ORDER.

On the other hand, FIRE FAILURE IS CAUSED BY PROGRESSING TOO FAR, TOO FAST. If you try and ignite a three foot, unsplit log with a match, you will not succeed, because big pieces of wood contain a lot of cold, which overcomes your puny heat source.

TINDER ⟶ KINDLING ⟶ FUEL

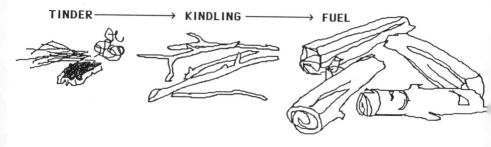

Take time and think your way through it. Memorize this code word to help you. S-PAD. Think:

SELECT a dry site, and dry wood.
PROPER PROGRESSION for proper burn.
AIR, plenty of, makes good fire.
DRY. Tinder, kindling, and wood.

How can you tell if wood is dry? Kindling bends when wet, snaps when dry. Thrown onto a rock, wet firewood thunks; if it's dry it knocks. Bark insulates so you can't get heat to the wood. Split kindling ignites much easier.

Site selection is important. On a hot summer day, building a cook-fire against dry logs or under a low hanging tree can surprise you worse than Gomer Pyle. On the other hand, if somebody is chasing you and the best you have is damp wood, tree branches will dissipate the smoke.

Proper progession starts witn an igniter, which catches softwood kindling, which ignites small pieces of fuel, to start your main fire. Building fire is often like boiling water. There you sit, dying of thirst, and you have to watch it do a rolling boil for 20 minutes. Who waits? Nobody. With a fire, there you kneel, colder than a landlord's heart, so you slop together a garbage heap of wet wood on snow, use all your firestarters and watch your hot hope flicker to cold despair. You're history.

HARDWOODS IGNITE HARD, BURN SLOW.
SOFTWOODS IGNITE EASY, BURN FAST.

What's a hardwood? To be ultimately correct, I have to go into a bodacious botanical explanation. Forget that. Just stick a knife into it. If it goes in easy, it's soft. Given a choice, use pitchy softwood for kindling. The pitch burns and adds great heat to your efforts.

Air plays a big part. Fires burn because of a chemical breakdown of your fuel in the presence of heat and OXYGEN. Jam your fuel too close together, and no air gets in so the fire smothers for lack of oxygen.

Once you have the fire going, here are some great ways to use it. Gather the heat into your body by making a reflector to RADIATE. Put two canteens full of hot water over your kidneys. Lots of blood passes through your kidneys, at the CONDUCTION point, so your whole body heats. Of course, drink some heat into your body with hot tea or soup. BREATHE across the top of the cup.

Of course, cooking is important, especially if you're dining on parasite-infested food. While I was in Okinawa, a marine drank a few beers too many and ate a raw snail. The parasites in the snail invaded his nervous system, and eventually his brain, and killed him. Had he roasted the little fella, it would've been nothing more than a tasty treat.

ALL COOKING UTENSILS FURNISHED COURTESY OF PERSONAL KNIFE AND GOD

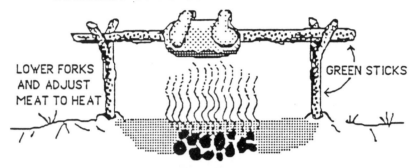

LOWER FORKS AND ADJUST MEAT TO HEAT

GREEN STICKS

IF YOU'RE TACTICAL, MAKE DRYWOOD FIRE DURING DAYLIGHT, WHICH BURNS DOWN TO HIDDEN (IN PIT) COALS FOR NIGHT TIME COOKING.

Some books teach you to use flames for some kinds of cooking. That's jive; use coals for everything. With coals, you can put any animal on a green-wood spit and cook it just right. Flames have to be watched closely because they shoot up everywhere, and burn anything in their way. Coals are safer, and you control the cooking heat by adjusting the distance between the coals and the meat.

Far above plenty of food, pure mountain water, great weather and good hunting---my favorite outdoor necessity is sleep. It cures the body of illness, creates a fresh brain that makes fewer judgment errors, sharpens the hunting senses, and gives you fast reflexes. Screw up sleeping, and several other problems will follow.

What's the basic? SLEEP WARM AND DRY.

134

Most humans fail to plan on sleeping warm by using a fire to ADD heat to the body. What most do is stand by the hot fire and cook one side of their body, then turn and cook the other while the formerly hot side, now turned away from the fire, re-freezes. When they tire of this dance, they crash and sleep.

Just before sunrise, it becomes coldest. The cold awakens them, and they try to build a fire. If they don't have enough wood gathered, they stuff their numb feet into frozen boots to go look for something burnable. It's the pits!

We think this is a better idea: In the morning, when you get up half frozen; you don't want to be making a fire--you want to stir the old one back to life. Treat your fire like money: Bank it. Do this by cutting down on the fire's air supply. Cover the hot coals with ashes and dirt. Then, in the morning, dig out a shovel-full of everything, and wobble the shovel in the wind. The ashes blow away, the sand sifts to the bottom, and the hot coals re-ignite fresh fuel to provide instant flame. If the coals aren't hot enough, or your morning fuel lacks kindling, manufacture a breeze, by cutting a canary reed to direct your breathe on the exact spot.

Here's another way: Stockpile enough wood to feed the fire all night long. Drink water just before hitting the sack so you set the alarm clock in your bladder. Then, as you drain your radiator, throw a couple of good dry logs on the fire, and go back to sleep.

Consider heating up some rocks in a fire. Hot rocks covered with sand will radiate warmth for a long time. You can take them inside a tight shelter and raise the temperature from biting cold

to semi-comfortable. You can also cover these with
sand under your bed. Heat rises; you will sleep a
lot warmer.

JAGGED EDGES

<<Don't; DO NOT, sit next to a   hot fire
with   river   bed   (nice,   smooth,   round
stones) heating up in the   coals.   River
bed rocks often contain pockets of water,
and severe heat makes enough steam to
cause the rocks to explode.   If that
happens, your friends will think you're
going to a movie show---as they notice you
spending a lot of time picking your
seat.>>

     In freezing weather, dig a spare trench and
make   sand/dirt piles next to it,   then leave some
extra   stones in the coals. If your bed goes   cold,
and you wake up, use your tongs to toss the hot
rocks   into the new trench, wipe the sand over   it,
and change beds to a new, warm one.

     Now,   here are the BRACE factors (IN   CAPS)
which fire will   reverse: BREATHING,maybe--across
hot liquids. RADIATION, Air Convection, CONDUCTION
(hot rock bed), and Evaporation.

     Conclusion..   Fire is fun,   good   for
cooking, a great morale factor, but NOT EVEN   CLOSE
TO SHELTER AS A HEAT SAVING DEVICE. So, read on...

Chapter 14

EFFICIENT SHELTER

We've just seen that only two, (perhaps 3) of the BRACE factors are reversed by using fire.

In contrast, what will shelter do?

Given warm air in your shelter, BREATHING, helps warm your body. Also, wind-breaker shelter stops RADIATION losses, as well as, AIR CONVECTION losses. See, no wind means no wind chill. Sleep off the ground or away from something really cold, and CONDUCTION won't bother you either. Finally, EVAPORATION doesn't happen in a shelter, because a decent roof over your head keeps you from getting wet. Basically, though, shelter keeps you warm in four out of five ways. Hot stuff.

Thus, it behooves you to be a shelter buildin' son-of-a-gun.

What should you build? The answer depends
on three factors:

HOW MUCH TIME DO YOU HAVE TO BUILD IT?
HOW LONG WILL YOU BE STAYING THERE?
WHAT MATERIALS ARE AVAILABLE?

Why build a palace for an overnight stay,
or a castle on a (warm) tropical island?   Once you
understand what you need, you know what you will
build, because form always follows function.

Frequently, weather or circumstance forces
you to build without enough time or material. Wait
too long in the day, or let a blizzard hit, and you
may have to build a place to live in a hurry.   We
call it hasty shelter; generally you won't use it
longer than a couple of nights.

Of course, portable shelter is an easy way
out. Think about a tent. Several light weight
backpack tents are available with a top covering,
called a fly, which keeps the rain out.

I favor tents with abundant windows.   In
hot climates, open windows provide cross
ventilation. You can also see through the mosquito
netting, and, if need be, shoot right through it.
Just patch the hole later.

Incidentally, don't buy bright colors.
Some tent makers use glamorous "granola" fabric;
the colors are either for nuts, flakes, or fruits.
Bright colors attract game wardens and forest
rangers, all of whom are in business to write
tickets.

In Oregon I talked with a couple of hunters
in Federal court. The crime: They built a fire
after a snow storm. The ranger wrote the ticket

because, even though we had an early snow, it was still "officially" fire season. I've had similar trouble with "burro-crats." So, go with camouflage, (or, at least forest green) and avoid trouble.

If you are a mobile nomad and you carry everything with you, a lightweight, backpack tent works just fine. But if you prefer to set up a base camp and work from there, you can spend a few hundred.

Knowing where to pitch your tent is more important than choosing a good one. Tents won't provide good shelter unless you choose an adequate campsite. Some of the possible hazards to consider are:

What if it rains?"
WATER RUN-OFF. Tents don't work too well under a waterfall, so don't park under a sloping rock shelf.
MUDSLIDE. Dirt banks close to a tent can create a disaster.

"What if it blows?"
HIGH WIND. You can tie your tent off against all kinds of wind, but why mess with it? Pick a site on the leeward side of a hill.
WIND BLOWN WOOD AND PINE CONES. Stay out of the edge of woodsy areas too, and look up for dead limbs, etc., before driving a tent stake.

"Who will become a close neighbor?"
SNAKES. Don't pitch your tent among rocks where a lot of mice and small rodents are present---snakes feed on them.
ANIMAL HAZARDS. Make sure to park your tent right over a whole bunch of elk or cow tracks. That way, sleep can turn into an exciting event. Just like humans, animals use and re-use the same trails frequently, and if anything scares & stampedes them, they don't bother to go around brush, small

trees, or canvas. You can't blame them, either. If you weighed 800 pounds, you'd go through anything.

CREEPY CRITTERS. Make it a habit to keep your tent closed tightly. My young son left my tent flap open during the day in a Hawaiian woods area, and a visiting centipede crawled across my nose at o'dark thirty one morning. In my sleep, I tried to brush him off. He bit me on the upper lip, and the pain was good training---for anybody who wants to prepare for Russian torture.

Before you build, consider what shelter materials you have available. Learn only a few, but be good at building with the ones you learn. Next, ask: "Why should shelter be built?" In other words, what BRACE factors am I trying to avoid? Think about it for just a moment, and you'll agree: the BRACE factors all operate more severely at night---and that's the time when you need MOST to be comfortable.

With only a little woods experience, you will learn this: Nothing at all will work as well for you as a good night's sleep. I've read a lot of outdoor books that tell you how to build all kinds of shelter, but that's the end of it. The author leaves you in a forest of shelter plans to fend for yourself. Somehow, you are supposed to crawl in and go to sleep. Where...? How...?

To answer these questions, I experimented-- a lot.
Obviously, you can't bring a bed with you into the woods. Even a cot gets to be heavy, so you are pretty much confined to sleeping on the ground with an ensolite pad or air mattress. But sleeping on the ground presents difficulties. First, you go to bed resting on a place where

140

snakes crawl around looking for a nice, warm, enclosed place. Also, overnight rains can flood you out. In cold weather, the ground frequently steals so much heat from your posterior that you wake up thinking you lost it.

There is a much better way to go: get above it all---with a hammock. Until you get used to them, however, they are mean. They dump you on the ground when you least expect it. I got good at using mine, but I watched a few times as some friends of mine absorbed a few hard landings, so I decided to find a better way to go.

After lots of testing in a lot of situations, I finally came up with the all-time winner. A sleep-anywhere-in-comfort, easy-to-carry, up, off-the-ground bed that can be used anywhere, anytime. It's cheap, too. Cost thirty cents.

FEED SACK ———
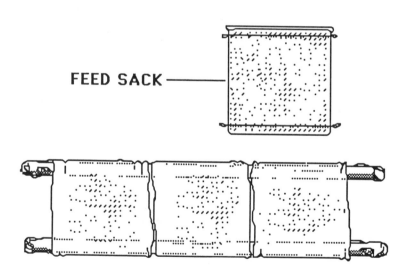

First, go out and buy your mattress. You purchase three feed sacks for ten cents each. The seams on each end of the sack will pull right out, leaving you with three hollow tubes. Fold and stuff these in your rucksack and you will always have a great bed with you.

You can cut a frame anywhere in the woods. Just cut a few reasonably straight branches out of a tree, then trim them down.

Suspend this bed above the ground in a number of ways:

A.   Prop it on four yoked sticks pounded into the ground.

B.   Bridge it against a tree trunk on one end, and use a hanger on the other.

C.   Build an A-frame that will accept the poles and spread them on each end.

HASTY SHELTERS

Use what's there. Cave. Rock overhang. Hollow Stump. Blown over tree. Snow bank. If you think you will need hasty shelter, it's a good idea to bring along some polyvinyl sheeting for covering a make-shift frame. In EVERYBODY'S KNIFE BIBLE we talked about utility to weight ratio. Polyvinyl sheeting fits the formula well. With only a little sunshine, it generates and contains warmth inside anything you build.

Think about fasteners. Without those vital little things, it will take forever to build a flop house. All of the old outdoor shelter books and theories employ rawhide and vines for lashing. A few talk about drilling holes and fitting dowels. More modern materials consist of nails, wire, parachute cord, rope/string, and tape. Personally, I like plastic ties. They are lightweight, strong, and bind anything in a jiffy.

GOING INTO THE SIDE OF A HILL

Cold? Winter coming and you're homeless? I can get you comfy in a few days. As I mentioned, Book II goes into individual training, and part of that outdoor training had to do with chainsaws. If you're in a hurry and you have a saw available, you can build a cordwood shelter into the side of a hill, and thus use mother earth as an insulator.

SHED ROOF

As you probably know, you can cut a cord of wood in a day. With a maul, split the round edges off to make it square. Once you have the edges square, you can stack them. Hopefully, you will have a few sacks of mortar mix so you stick them together with feeling.

Lay the squared cordwood on top of one another. Notice the rebar used to hold the corners together. If you don't have steel, inter-lock the ends by alternating them.

From the side, the cordwood structure should stand on its own. Before you back-fill, use rocks (and pipe, if you have it) to set a drainage ditch. That way, you will keep water pressure (mud) from pressing against the structure. Note also, the moisture seal used on the outside of the wall; it's poly-vinyl here, and the thicker it is, the better.

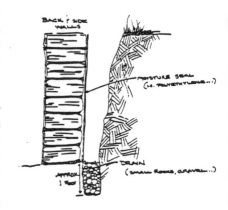

THE LEAN-TO

This is a popular hasty shelter. I like it because the materials required can be found in ANY woodsy area. Besides, add-ons are easy. If you decide to stay where you are, you can increase living space without having to start all over. One way of doing that, of course, is to build another lean-to, and join the two of them at the top. The result: An A-Frame.

Rather than carry a tent into and out of the woods, I like building a lean-to. Building a fire close to a tent is risky, (flash fire) but a lean-to made from wet wood won't ignite unless you almost torch it, so a contained fire is a safe bet.

Books that teach lean-to's overlook some key points. First, cut all similar pieces at the same time, then lay them out and build the sections on the ground for speed. Second, make your lean-to adjustable. With only a little extra effort, you can raise or lower the whole structure so that it will either shed snow, act as a better windbreak, or drop down to contain more heat.

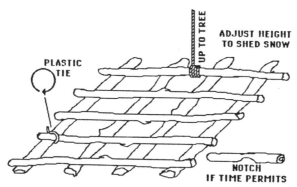

Once you have the lean-to built and tied in place, think about adding on. Consider side support posts to take the strain off the support ropes.

If you want more heat reflected inside and you have some aluminum foil wrap with you, take a half hour or so to make this addition. Then lower your lean-to almost all the way back to the ground and attach it.

Build side walls next. Build them on the ground also, and tilt them into position.

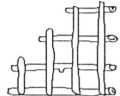

Lean-to's can last a long time. Also, because you only have a few walls to build, they can be built in a hurry. For a week or less, it's the shelter I would choose.

SEMI-PERMANENT SHELTERS

If you have food and good water handy, you might decide to stay a while. With plenty of time, and desire for convenience, you can build a classic castle. Assuming you decide to stay for awhile, you will need something more permanent.

First: Take into account the local climate changes. I just came back from Fiji, an island in the South Pacific, where I researched construction. The climate there is hot, so insulated walls and steep roofs (to shed snow) are unnecessary.

In parts of Australia, it is equally warm. There, however, you need to build more of a castle because of highly poisonous tree climbing snakes.

Second: Look at the materials you have available. In Fiji I had a lot of volcanic rock and small trees, mingled with some bigger trees. In 80% of the places you might find yourself, trees and rocks will be the case.

CASTLES IN THE SKY

You can build wickiups, cabins, rock houses, and underground-cave combinations, but for me, nothing beats a tree house.

Until recently, they haven't been too popular, though. They were dangerous to build; you had to hang in a tree like a baboon to start one. Also, getting a platform level on branches that run all over is tricky. Finally, tree strength can be problem.

But we've solved these problems, and we'll show you how. Let's think first about weight. Many of us have had experience breaking limbs and breaking limbs. The first belonged to a tree, and the second was ours. Ouch!

You need to know that anything you build in a tree won't crash to the ground. So, the first step in building is to determine how much weight the tree's limbs will hold.

You can do this by hanging a large water-holding vessel, such as a 50 gallon drum, on the limb you trust the least. Tie off the free end of the rope to the trunk of another tree, and then slowly fill the drum with water. Since 50 gallons of water weigh about 400 pounds, you know the limb will hold that weight. Once the limbs are tested, you are ready to build.

Even though you know all the limbs are strong, hang most of your structure weight on the trunk of the tree, so that the load is a compression load, rather than a bending or twisting one on the outer limbs. You want the structure supported from the trees strength; the outer limbs should be used only to provide stability.

Work safely. Use a Baker (brand name) tree stand to set a temporary platform so you don't risk falling. Use a safety rope to hold you in case you slip or fall. For the best attachment to your body, try a Swiss seat (made from rope) or a good commercial seat made from nylon. (Brigade Quartermaster Catalog Sales, Marietta, Georgia).

Now, how can we attach finished lumber or hand carved (straight) lumber to the tree? That's the critical question. You can't use nails or spikes too successfully; some of them kill trees. Lag bolts are out for the same reason.

Another vital factor in tree house attachment, however, is the adjustability factor. Trees grow, and you may need to adjust your floor supports from time to time in order to keep your house level.

To solve all of these problems, bore a half inch hole completely through each of your support limbs. All the holes have to be the same height, so use a clear plastic hose filled with water. No matter where you pull the hose, the two water marks on the inside will stay level. Once you have drilled them all, spray the insides of the holes with tree paint to prevent insects from eating your foundation.

Now, bolt on either 2X6 or 3X6 blocks, with the grain HORIZONTAL to the ground. Once you have these bolted on the tree, you can put your main floor stringers on top of them, and bolt the stringers together (not through the tree) to compress on the trunk above the supports. As always with bolts, use large washers between the wood and the bolt heads or nuts. Don't tighten these too tightly; you only want to rest on your

block supports, not smash the tree. As the tree
grows and the limbs thicken, loosen the bolts.

If you can get tongue and groove (T&G)
lumber for flooring, use that. It will distribute
a load over a longer span. Even so, 6 ft is about
maximum.

MAKE SURE TO CANTILEVER YOUR FLOOR TWO FEET
OR MORE OVER THE EDGE OF YOUR SUPPORT BEAMS.   You
will need the space on the deck later.

From a level floor, cut limbs to create the
view of a lifetime. A long pole with a pull saw
will remove any obstructions in the way of your
view.   Remember, though, that if you can see out
clearly, others can see in.

Once your platform is level, you can put
your tent on it and enjoy life as you should.
Then, later, if you need sturdier shelter, you can
build walls and a roof on the platform with a
lightweight material.   Be sure and build all the
walls to the same height. That way, you will have
an easy time with the roof. As with tents, tree
houses should have windows. I prefer plastic over
glass because it's lighter.   Remember, heavy
materials put a strain on your tree.

Build a pointed roof to accommodate
snowfall. Corrugated tin roofing is great if snows
a lot. In tropics the roof can be flatter. Paint,
and then wax the outside of your roofing material
on the ground before you put it up, and a little
heat will cause the snow to slide off easily. In a
tropical climate, corrugated Fiberglas will do just
fine; you're only concerned with rain.

Finally, you will need access to your
tree house. Getting up and down can be a chore,

especially with a load of groceries.

Think about an elevator. Several good 12
volt winches are available. With house current,
(from any generator), you use a battery charger and
the 12 v. system operates the winch. Using several
wraps on the bottom spindle and the top spindle,
install a continuous line from top to bottom. On
that line, tie off several butterfly loops so you
have a place to insert a foot. Then, hang on to
the rope, and winch-lift yourself and your baggage
into heaven.

You can also install a ladder, or, if
you're strong and enjoy rope climbing, you merely
use spaced knots on a rope from the top to the
ground. In that case, you can take the rope in at
night and enjoy freedom from intrusion.

No matter what method you use to get up
into the tree house, make sure to run the stairs
or elevator up past the floor level so that
stepping into the house is an easy, level chore.

We could teach every kind of shelter known
to man. Somebody already did that when they wrote,
SHELTER SHACKS AND SHANTIES, which has recently re-
appeared in print.

But knowing how to build everything doesn't
matter. What's important is knowing the reasons
why. Learning just a few kinds of shelter will
cover you just about anywhere in the world. Thus,
no matter where you go or what you do, you will be
able to establish yourself in a great place to
live.

This is an early copy of
THE GREEN BERET'S COMPASS COURSE.

Now pocket-sized, perfect bound, and also with camouflage cover. Take this booklet into the woods with you and you will:

Never get lost again!

Throw out all your maps; you won't need them.

Bee-line straight back to camp. You will never need to go the long way by back-tracking again.

Scare your friends out of their wits as you travel ground they haven't seen before, neglect to carry a map, and land them right on base with no trouble at all.

$6.95

Mail order from:

PATHFINDER PUBLICATIONS

150 HAMAKUA DR / #401, KAILUA, HAWAII 96734

THE GREEN BERETS
GUIDE TO OUTDOOR SURVIVAL

INDEX

What Makes These Books the BEST?

Never Before ...

. . . has Green Beret technique and know-how been made public!

. . . has any author travelled all over the world to interview Green Berets and get the best!

. . . have so many photos and illustrations dropped outdoor knowledge in your lap!

WE AT PATHFINDER . . .

. . . publish new and novel methods for real outdoorsmen. Since 1982, we have sold thousands of outdoor books containing systems and methods used by the best woodsmen in the United States.

PATHFINDER PUBLICATIONS
Hamakua Center, Suite 401
150 Hamakua Drive
Kailua, Oahu, Hawaii 96734

ABOUT THE
AUTHOR/EDITOR

Sgt. Don Paul began winning trophies for long range rifle shooting as soon as he entered the Army. He later became a top competition shooter/coach at 6th Army matches.

Later on, in Special Forces, he retired from the Army when his career came to a sudden halt — due to parachute failure.

He has since travelled all over the world and gathered the very best in outdoor techniques from personal friends and fellow soldiers, the Green Berets.

His outdoor books have sold everywhere; they reveal never-before released tricks and tips for getting along in style in the woods.

Use This Convenient Coupon
To Order These Books . . .

Please send me:

☐ **EVERYBODY'S KNIFE BIBLE**
at **$9.95** . . . . _____ copies
Green Beret Methods and Knife Mannerisms. Don't buy a knife until
you've read this book! It teaches you to use your knife for vital outdoor
skills, including night travel, navigation, river crossing, foraging and
defense. Plus a lot more!

☐ **THE GREEN BERET'S GUIDE TO OUTDOOR SURVIVAL**
at **$12.95** . . . . _____ copies
. . . by a special team of Green Berets. This includes inside information on
the Green Beret Team Concept; new, simple teachings on hand-to-hand
combat; how to double your survive-ability; and SUPER SHOOTER —
all new shooting concepts that make your guns speak with ultimate
authority.

☐ **GREAT LIVIN' IN GRUBBY TIMES**
at **$12.95** . . . . _____ copies
. . . Volume II makes the reader an outdoor expert. See how the Green
Berets choose a Survival Firearm; Make Handmade Weapons; pick a
Survival Habitat; and then outfit with Great Gear for Grubby Times.
Finally, build shelter and furniture with a Chainsaw; then defend it with
Combat Gunnery.

☐ **GREEN BERET'S COMPASS COURSE**
at **$6.95** . . . . _____ copies
. . . Thousands sold since 1983 and fast becoming the land navigation
system of the future for all outdoorsmen, this handbook keeps you from
EVER getting lost in the woods. Requires no maps and shoots you
straight back home by the shortest route possible. A life-saver that gives
you better directional sense than a desert coyote.

☐ *Special!* **BOOKS I & II**
at **$19.95** for both . . . . _____ sets

☐ *Special!* **BOOKS I, II & COMPASS COURSE**
at **$24.95** for all three . . . . _____ sets

☐ *Special!* **BOOKS I, II & KNIFE BIBLE**
at **$27.95** for all three . . . . _____ sets

☐ *Special!* **ALL FOUR BOOKS**
at **$32.95** for all four . . . . _____ sets

MONEY-BACK GUARANTEE

Name _____

Address _____

**Phone (   ) _____

Send order form and check or money order to:
PATHFINDER PUBLICATIONS
Hamakua Center, Suite 401
150 Hamakua Drive
Kailua, Oahu, Hawaii 96734

Book II . . .

GREAT LIVIN' IN GRUBBY TIMES

Everybody's Outdoor Life Made Easy!
Tips and tricks from Green Berets!

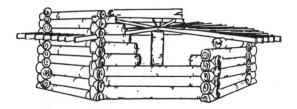

CHOOSE A SURVIVAL FIREARM — Make the super perfect personal selection after learning from the Green Berets.

STARTING FROM SCRATCH-CHAINSAW Use this tool in new, inventive ways to produce a well-heated castle and all its furniture.

WATER, PLENTIFUL AND PURE — How to obtain, and then purify water to keep your whole team healthy.

HANDMADE WEAPONS — What to do without guns.

ESCAPE AND EVASION Taught by America's number one expert.

WHAT TO TAKE WITH YOU — The Green Beret writing team gives you the list of outdoor items and all necessary tools and implements.

SURVIVAL HABITAT — Choosing a place to survive has a lot to do with whether you succeed or fail.

134 PAGES, SOFTCOVER ISBN # 0-938263-02-1
ILLUSTRATED $12.95